The Good,
the Spam,
and the Ugly

THE
GOOD
THE
SPAM
AND THE
UGLY

Shooting It Out with Internet Bad Guys

Steve Graham

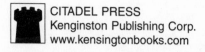

CITADEL PRESS
Kenginston Publishing Corp.
www.kensingtonbooks.com

CITADEL PRESS BOOKS are published by

Kensington Publishing Corp.
850 Third Avenue
New York, NY 10022

All Kensington titles, imprints, and distributed lines are available at special quantity discounts for bulk purchases for sales promotions, premiums, fund-raising, educational, or institutional use. Special book excerpts or customized printings can also be created to fit specific needs. For details, write or phone the office of the Kensington special sales manager: Kensington Publishing Corp., 850 Third Avenue, New York, NY 10022, attn: Special Sales Department; phone 1-800-221-2647.

CITADEL PRESS and the Citadel logo are Reg. U.S. Pat. & TM Off.

First printing: March 2007

10 9 8 7 6 5 4 3 2 1

Printed in the United States of America

Library of Congress Control Number: 2006935119

ISBN-13: 978-0-8065-2824-3
ISBN-10: 0-8065-2824-9

For Mom.

Don't worry; I used a pseudonym.

*************************Contents*************************

You, the public, should be grateful for this book. Because it signals the beginning of my professional writing career, which means society now has one less lawyer. I know giving lawyers book contracts is an expensive, inefficient way of getting rid of them, but at least it's legal. You may not realize it, but many backward states still have laws against the extermination and/or composting of attorneys. It's generally a misdemeanor punishable by up to half a day of picking up dog droppings in a public park, or a fine which could run into the dozens of dollars. Not that it wouldn't be worth it.

Furthermore, the careless disposal of used attorneys may violate local environmental protection laws concerning hazardous waste.

Anyway, as I thrill the profession by making my exit, I want to thank a few people in order to convey the misleading impression that I am not an ingrate who expects to have everything handed to him.

First, my agent, John Talbot. I was thinking about giving up on writing when he contacted me out of the blue. He had faith in me when most people—especially those who know me best—thought I was a hopeless goof who ought to be given a charity stipend and placed in some sort of walled facility. It is still not clear which view of the situation is the better one, but at least now I have a chance to prove I should be allowed to remain at large and relatively unmedicated.

Second, my editor, Gary Goldstein. He is the kind of editor writers dream about. The kind who doesn't seek out signs of quality in a writer's work in order to remove them. He has been a tremendous supporter and a loyal advocate, which is why I hope I can do more projects with him in the future. That may not sound like high praise, but it is. Generally I fantasize about running editors through mulching equipment.

Third, my father. His support has been invaluable. And I appreciate him not running into the yard and throwing a screaming tantrum in front of the neighbors when I decided to quit practicing. That being said, he needs to give up his dream of living in the Virgin Islands and having me support him. Work is good for old people. Keeps the mind clear and prevents them from forming gangs and loitering in malls.

I wish my late mother could be here to see my book sitting on the shelves at local stores. Although I am not sure I would want her reading the chapter about the South African transvestite.

Thanks to everyone who has supported my work over the last few years and given me encouragement. A share of the credit for my success belongs to you. I only wish I could also share the liability for any legal problems to which it gives rise.

Enjoy the book. And if it offends you and you decide to hunt me down and give me a beating, please have the grace to alert me and give me a ten-minute head start.

And please, no cutting in line.

The Good,
the Spam,
and the Ugly

Date: Thu, 8 Sep 2005 12:11:58 -0700 (PDT)
From: "Steve H." <xxxx@yahoo.com>
Subject: Re: VERY URGENT FOR ME NOW PLEASE
To: fatima_a_rasheed@yahoo.com

Dear Fatima:
Let me extend my sympathy on the loss of your husband and the problems with your cancerous breasts. Allow me to point out something that may bring you comfort. Judging from your age, it would appear that by the time your breasts became diseased, your husband had already gotten a lifetime of gratifying use from them.

I am quite eager to participate in your deal. You say you want the money to go to the less privileged. I can't hardly think of anyone who fits that description better than me. Until recently, I was the Des Moines area's leading pet psychic. But I was run out of town after doing a reading on the mayor's Chihuahua. Perhaps you are familiar with these dogs. In appearance, they resemble a large balding rodent, and in Mexico, their tender flesh forms the basis for a number of tasty dishes.

In any case, I made the mistake of reading the mayor's Chihuahua after ingesting an unfortunate combination of chocolate martinis and a homemade antidepressant derived from the root of the Jimson weed, and in front of the entire Rotary Club, I stated that the dog was distressed by the mayor's penchant for pornographic DVDs involving the abuse of sedated livestock.

Shortly thereafter, my trailer was burned to the ground, and I was made to understand that I would be wise to relocate. I currently reside in an abandoned cement mixer, where I sustain myself by laboring as a freelance sex worker catering to the transient trade.

Let me know what has to be done, and I will gladly do it. Whatever it is, I assure you that in the recent past, I have stooped even lower. And before that, I was a building contractor.

Steve Hopkins
Foosball, West Carolina

I'm sure it has happened to you.

You're sitting at your desk, trying not to let your boss catch you viewing Internet porn, when an e-mail arrives from a far-off land, usually a country in Africa. The subject line is capitalized. It says something like CONTACT ME ASAP or TREAT WITH IMPORTANCE or EMERGENCY CONSIGNMENT.

You open it, and lo and behold, it's the opportunity of a lifetime. Some corrupt Nigerian general has been poisoned by his own troops. Or a wealthy businessman has been killed in a plane crash, usually in Scotland or, alternatively, "Scottland." And there is a huge pile of money waiting to be claimed, if only some honest American like yourself will come forward and pose as the next of kin.

Congratulations. You've been selected to become a mugu.

"Mugu" is an expression African con artists use to describe the remarkable people who are stupid enough to fall for these e-mails, yet somehow intelligent enough to read and write and operate computers. And they really do exist.

Just like the sad folks who buy time shares. Or the ones who think three-card Monte is a real game. Or the ones who proudly insisted the famous Palm Beach ballot was too complicated for them to read.

The crooks get their bank information and so on, and the first thing you know, the hapless mugus find themselves not only stupid, but broke.

Because the supply of suckers is so great, there are now mansions in Nigeria belonging to pus-oozing dirt merchants who do nothing but milk mugus. Lagos supposedly has an upscale suburb full of spam mansions.

Nigeria has laws, believe it or not, and the mugu problem is so severe they have passed a law penalizing mugu abusers. This law is known as Section 419, and the wealthy gentlemen who make their money violating it are known as 419 scammers. And they're not all from Nigeria or even Africa, even though I myself tend to use the word "Nigerian" to describe all members of the class. Lately, I've been getting a lot of e-mails purporting to be from China and Russia.

The incredible thing about 419 scammers is that even though they do quite well, they are amazingly, astoundingly gullible. You can tell them just about anything, and they swallow it like bums swarming on a trough full of cheap wine.

Guess how I found that out.

Like many folks who frequent the Internet, I eventually got tired of deleting mugu mail, and I decided to turn the tables on the crooks. I send them e-mails that become increasingly ridiculous until they finally realize I'm yanking their chains.

I never respond in my own name. That's no fun at all, and it's also dangerous. I come up with wonderful aliases. Sometimes I'm a randy widow who inherited a profitable company that manufactures hemorrhoid clamps. Whatever those are. Sometimes I'm a lonely guy who got maimed by a pin-setting machine in a bowling alley. Sometimes I'm Ernest Hemingway. Once I even convinced a spammer my name was "Mr. Toilet Seat." Pronounced "Twah-let SAY-ot." Mr. Seat is from Thailand.

There are recurrent themes in my e-mails. Things I can't help inserting, again and again. Mongooses appear frequently, as do midgets. And the Flintstones. Don't ask me why.

I like working bits of American culture into my work. I tell the spammers my name is Wile E. Coyote, and that my lawyer's name is Elmer Fudd. I tell them Anne B. Davis was our Secretary of State during the Franco-American War, and that she also invented the cotton gin. I tell them about my personal physicians, Dr. Scholl and Dr. McCoy. And none of this ever fazes them. Some of my exchanges have gone on for months.

There are other people who torture 419 spammers. And some of them get more work out of them than I do. They get more photos and so on, and some of these folks actually get spammers to send *them* money. That's fine, but that's not really my shtick. Getting photos and making the spammers do stupid things is sort of peripheral. My primary goal is to have a good time writing this stuff. This book is the result.

Note for the Incorrigibly PC

The vast majority of spammers I've abused have been—or have claimed to be—black Africans. For that reason, I know I'm in danger of being vilified by self-righteous simpletons who get off on accusing other people of racism. Let me tell you a few things before you make complete asses of yourselves.

1. I didn't choose the people who tried to swindle me. They chose me. If they had all been from Canada, this book would be about Canadians. It's not my fault most of them are African. I take what comes. When I had the opportunity, I worked on spammers claiming to be from other countries, but the simple fact is, they were a lot harder to fool. Don't blame me. Blame the Nigerian school system.

2. If I said things in my e-mails you think are offensive, you have to remember, I'm always playing a character. Part of the fun is seeing how far these idiots will go to get along with a tremendous clod.

3. By and large, 419 scammers are vicious, ruthless criminals. It is estimated that innocent Americans send them a million dollars per day. Some individuals have lost their life savings to 419 spammers. Others have been lured to Africa and beaten and robbed and even killed by these people. And the network extends inside the United States; foreign criminals have come to the homes of 419 victims right here in America, issuing threats of violence. Believe it or not, I may have put myself in danger by writing this book.

Meanwhile, in Nigeria, the crimes of 419 thugs are openly celebrated. There's actually a hit song over there called "I Will Eat Your Dollars," making fun of the hapless folks who've been taken in by spamming degenerates.

As far as I'm concerned, I'm doing God's work. If you sympathize with the criminals, you have some pretty sick values. I make no apologies for the fun I've had tormenting these pinheads.

With that behind me, I present a selection of e-mails for your amusement and edification. They are all absolutely real. Read, enjoy, and learn.

Steve and Stephanie sat on the verandah, sipping Smirnoff Ice and complaining about the flightiness of Nigerians. "They can't be real men. They must be women," said Stephanie. "No real man could resist all THIS." She raised her arms, making the fat beneath them swing like saloon doors with spider veins.

"I know how you feel, sis," said Steve. "I invited a refugee girl to come live with me, and she didn't even write back. A dang REFUGEE."

"There's no accounting for taste," said Stephanie. She drained the bottle, tossed it into the bushes, and scratched a breast which lay somewhere to her left. "No," said Steve, scraping a scab with the key to his orange Pontiac Aztek. "There certainly ain't."

Before getting into the longer and more complicated exchanges, I think I ought to show you a few shorter ones to get you into the mood. I've strung some spammers along for weeks and months, but often they wise up after the first or second e-mail and I never hear from them again. That's a shame, because I've wasted really fine material on guys who ran off before I could get cranking.

I'll give you general guidelines to help you keep everything straight in your mind. Where you see "[SNIP]" or an ellipsis, I cut material I thought was superfluous or tedious. And **boldface always indicates material i wrote,** even if it appears to be from a 419 spammer. Finally, I'll always alter or omit my e-mail address. I don't want readers sending me their "humorous" fake 419 e-mails to see if they can get me to respond. Finally, my publisher's lawyers advised me to alter the e-mail addresses of the spammers. So I did.

Take a deep breath. I'm going to reprint an entire message from a guy in Senegal. He calls himself "Keita Duoala." Kind of makes your face hurt to say it.

From "Keita Duoala" <keitaduoala@xxx.az>
To: "xxxxxxx" <xxxxxxx@yahoo.com>
Subject: CAN YOU BE TRUSTED?

FOREIGN REMITTANCE DEPARTMENT.
BANK OF AFRICA (B.O.A.)
DAKAR.
Tel;+2215959694

My Dear Friend,

I am Mr. Duoala Keita the Director of bill and exchange at the foreign remittance department of BANK OF AFRICA (B.O.A) Senegal. In my department we discovered an abandoned sum of $5.5m in an account that belongs to one of our foreign customer (ENGINEER CHRISTAIN EICH) who died along with his wife and two sons and his wife's parents on a Monday, 31 July, 2000, 13:22 GMT in a plane crash.

http://news.bbc.co.uk/1/hi/world/europe/859479.stm

Since we got information about his death, we have been expecting his next of kin to come over and claim his money because we cannot release it unless some body applies for it as next of kin or relation to the deceased as indicated in our banking guidlings and laws but unfortunately we learnt that all his supposed next of kin died alongside with him at the plane crash leaving nobody behind for the claim. It is therefore upon this discovery that I now decided to make this business proposal to you and release the money to you as the next of kin to the deceased for safety and subsequent disbursement since nobody is coming for it and we don't want this money to go into the bank treasury as unclaimed bill.

The banking laws and guidlines here stipulates that if such money remained unclaimed after fours years, the money will be transfered into the bank treasury as unclaimed fund. The request of foreigner as next of kin in this business is occassioned by the fact that the customer was a foreigner.

I agree that 30% of this money will be for you as a respect to the provision of a foriegn account, 10% will be set aside for expenses incurred during the business and 60% would be for me Thereafter, I will visit your country for disbursement according to the percentage indicated. Therefore, to enable the immediate transfer of this fund to you, your private telephone and fax number for easy and effective communication is very important. I will not fail to bring to your notice this transaction is hitch-free and that you should not entertain any attom of fear as all required arrangements have been made for smooth and succesful transfer. You should contact me immediately as soon as you receive this letter. Trusting to hearing from you.

Yours Sincerely,
Duoala Keita.

I am showing it in its entirety because it's very typical of the genre. A plane crash. A URL. And a lovely mound of cash, waiting to be claimed. I took it very seriously, as you will see.

Date: Wed, 7 Sep 2005 14:34:05 -0700 (PDT)
From: "Steve H." <xxxxxxx@yahoo.com>

Subject: Re: CAN YOU BE TRUSTED?
To: "Keita Duoala" <keitaduoala@xxx.az>

Dear Mr. or Ms. Duoala:
Your letter is somewhat confusing. Are you saying you had a customer whose first name was Engineer? My second cousin Evadna named her son Barber because she liked the music from the movie "Platoon," but Engineer is a new one on me.

In any case, while I am highly interested in your deal, I must ask up front if it is strictly legal. The reason I am asking is that I am currently serving a suspended sentence for releasing several monkeys that were being used in trials for a drug intended to enlarge the private parts of unfortunate gentlemen.

I acted out of mercy, as the drug worked quite well, and these animals were lonely and frustrated because the other monkeys had become frightened of them. I now regret my impulsive action, as these deformed primates are running loose and have eased their frustration by assaulting a number of helpless cats and a bantam rooster, which later had to be put down.

The rooster's owner was so mad she threatened to tie me to a picnic bench and bait the area with sliced bananas.

Steve Hopkins
Bartertown, DE

Maybe his response will help you understand how easy it is to toy with these boobs. You have to wonder what Africans think of America to buy a story like that.

Date: Thu, 8 Sep 2005 06:50:11 -0700 (PDT)
From: "Keita Duoala" <keitaduoala@xxx.az>

Subject: Re: CAN YOU BE TRUSTED?
To: xxxxxxx@yahoo.com

Dear Steve,
I appreciate your acceptance and willingness to assist me in this transaction. I hope you understood my message (please read my first e-mail again). First what you/we have to do is to include your name in the data base of next of kin, so that it will appear and fit you in as the true beneficiary/next of kin to the late Christian Eich. Secondly, legal documents would have to be procured in your name, this is because i want everything to be LEGAL.

However, to commence the transaction/process, I would want you to respond immediatly with:

1. your full names

2. Phone and fax numbers

3. your full address

These information are needed so as to be imputed into our data base for authentic clearification when verified.

Call me on: +221 595 9694.

Regards,
D. Keita.

I figured Keita would want an update on the monkeys and their sexual exploits. It's too bad they were imaginary. It would be great to load them into a truck and release them at certain types of functions. Sexual harassment seminars. PETA fund-raisers. Anything involving Dr. Phil. (You have to love a big fatass who charges people for dieting advice.)

Date: Thu, 8 Sep 2005 10:43:37 -0700 (PDT)
From: "Steve H." <xxxxxxx@yahoo.com>

Subject: Re: CAN YOU BE TRUSTED?
To: "Keita Duoala" <keitaduoala@xxx.az>

Dear Keith:
I thought the joy of releasing seven dozen hormonally altered monkeys would be a hard experience to top, but receipt of your fine e-mail is more stirring by far.

I am wondering now if I misread your original message; however, as to the best of my knowledge, I am not related to any persons named Eich. I hope you will forgive me if I appear to be casting aspersions, but it sort of looks like you want me to PRETEND to be related to this Eich character. Is that the case? If so, I need some time to think. If pretending to be related to a dead person is a crime, I would have to be assured that I would only be breaking Senegalese law, which as we all know is kind of a farce. Breaking American law is a much bigger deal, as I would certainly be forced to go to prison for the remainder of my monkey sentence.

You request my full names, but I only have the one. My name is Steven Ignatius Hopkins. My address is 21 Jump Street, Bartertown, Delaware 19801.

Last night, one of the monkeys surprised a town alderman who happens to be an achondroplastic dwarf, and before the alderman fought him off, he managed to get to "third base." I hope they are recaptured soon, as they clearly pose a threat to the virtue of unescorted height-challenged citizens.

I did offer to pay for the dry cleaning.

Steve Hopkins
Bartertown, DE

Keita was pretty sharp for a spammer. He dropped me like a hot banana. Potato, I mean.

As long as I'm showing you bits of exchanges which have been partially destroyed, let me drag out some correspondence between Mrs. Stella Sigcau and one of my less-plausible aliases. I lost her original e-mail, but believe it or not, spammer e-mails get such wide distribution, you can usually find them by using a search engine. People post them on websites. I found the following text using Google. It's probably what Mrs. Sigcau sent me. I wish I still had her photo. She bore a striking resemblance to Florida Evans from *Good Times*.

FROM MRS. STELLA SIGCAU,
Minister of Public Works, South Africa

DEAR SIR/MA,

REQUEST FOR URGENT BUSINESS ASSISTANCE
After due deliberation with my children, I decided to contact you for your assistance in standing as a beneficiary to the sum of US30.5M Thirty Million, Five Hundred Thousand United States Dollars Only)

First, let me start by introducing myself as Mrs. Stella Sigcau, a mother of three children and the Minister of Public Works in South African Government (17 June 1999) to date under the auspices of the President of South Africa MR THABO MBEKI. You can view my profile at my website:
http://www.gov.za/gol/gcis_profile.jsp?id=1068

THE PROPOSAL
After the swearing in ceremony making me the Minister of Public Works in South African Government (17 June 1999), my husband Mr Edelebe Sigcau died while he was on an official trip to Trinidad and Tobago in 1996. After his death, I discovered that he had some funds in a dollar account which amounted to the sum of US$30.5M with a Financial Institution

[SNIP—You get the idea, right? I don't have to show you the entire 3,000-word pitch.]

Thanks for your anticipated co-operation and my regards to your family.

Yours faithfully,
MRS. STELLA SIGCAU,

Minister of Public Works,
South Africa

Poor Stella. Her husband was dead, and she had three kids to raise. And now she was looking for help from a beer-buzzed American jackass pretending to be a cartoon character.

Dear Mrs. Sigcau:

What straits you must be in, trying to raise three children all by yourself. I am sure 30 million dollars would be very helpful, and I would like to see you get it. I myself was raised by a single mother. I was one of six children, born in the Mojave Desert. Sometimes we were so poor we had to eat wild game such as the small birds known as roadrunners. When we could catch them.

I could use the money, too, as my company, Acme Products, is in a slump due to the passing of restrictive laws regarding the sale of fireworks, large magnets, and anvils.

Also, I have medical problems resulting from a traffic accident. Some prankster redirected the line on a local highway, and I followed it into the side of a mesa.

Please let me know what must be done.

Wile E. Coyote
Needles, CA

Unfortunately, I no longer have the next two e-mails, but I can give you the gist. Stella was overjoyed to learn that a fine American businessman wanted to help her. Mr. Coyote wrote her back, saying he wanted to use her money to promote a new product he had invented. Stella sent him another e-mail to string him along, and she expressed her sympathies regarding his painful injuries.

Then Mr. Coyote wanted to see if he could get her to send a funny picture, so he sent her the following message.

Dear Ms. Sigcau:

Thank you for your response and your sympathy. My injuries from running into the side of the mesa were painful but not life threatening. I am getting better, although for a while I felt as though an anvil had been dropped on me.

You may leave a message on my portable telephone, at 305-xxx-xxxx. There is a good chance that I will not be able to answer, as I spend a good part of the day testing new Acme products. But I do return calls.

My address is:

Wile E. Coyote
1957 Runner Road
Needles, CA 92363

If you wish to go forward, I need some evidence that you are serious and honest. I would appreciate a recent photo.

Because there are many duplicitous individuals using the Internet, I cannot accept a photo unless it is unquestionably recent and genuine. Therefore, I ask that you send a photo—nothing fancy, mind you—of yourself holding a paper with the name of my attorney on it. His name is Elmer Fudd.

Of course, I shall send you my photo as well.

I truly look forward to doing business with you.

Wile E. Coyote
Needles, CA

I sent her the passport I always send these idiots. I found a photo of a real passport, and I put Al Franken's picture on it, and I carefully forged the name "Wile E. Coyote" in the appropriate locations. Here it is, with the photo removed to prevent me from being sued by Al Franken or the person who took the original photo.

I never got the Fudd photo. You can always tell when one of these idiots doesn't have a camera. She stalled me. And she made a reference to my fabulous new invention.

Dear Mr Wile E. Coyote,

I took out time to study my correspondences with you and i can't find no place where Mr. Fudd Elmer comes in. I wonder if you were reffering to my hunsband Late Mr. Edelebe Sigcau who is the depositor of the funds. You have been sincere to me by giving me youe indentification as such i will forward my husband identification upon your request and the evidence of the deposit. I intend to also forward my driving indetification also.

What exactly do you mean by **magnetic bird seed**? could you furninsh me with more information on your company the benefit and risk of investing in your firm. Are there market for your products? Though my investment would come when you claim the fund anyway.

Thank you.

Sincerely,
Mrs. Sigcau.

She got all huffy when I said I really wanted that photo, so I cut her loose.

Here's a good example of a short exchange featuring my most active alias, Stephanie Hopkins. She's the amorous widow I mentioned in the Introduction. A while back, she got the following e-mail from Eloy Savimbi, of Angola.

From: "Eloy Savimbi" <e_savimbi456@yahoo.co.uk>
To: Stephanie Hopkins
Subject: YOUR ASSISTANCE IS NEEDED URGENTLY !!!!!!

Dear Sir, madam.

This letter may come to you as a surprise due to the fact that we have not met before i managed to get your contact details through the internet myself, Time is of importance and I was desperately looking for a person to assist me in this confidential transaction.

My movement and that of other members of my family have been highly restricted but happily I have been able to escape out of Angola and am now in London United Kingdom. I am Eloy Sakiata Savimbi, son of the late leader of Unita Rebel Jonas Savimbi of Angola who died on the 22nd February 2002. (http://www.empereur.com/angola.html) Before the death of my father he deposited the sum of USD15,000,000.00 (fifteen million United States dollars) in a private security trust company for safe keeping only.

[SNIP]

PLEASE YOUR CONFIDENTIALITY IN THIS TRANSACTION IS HIGHLY REQUIRED.

Yours sincerely,

Eloy Savimbi
Note: You can contact me on this phone number +44-703-1956-384
e_savimbi456@yahoo.co.uk

Stephie sometimes has interesting deformities. I thought I'd create a really good one for Eloy. She had a problem spelling his name.

Date: Tue, 13 Sep 2005 13:11:26 -0700 (PDT)
From: "Stephanie Hopkins"

Subject: Re: YOUR ASSISTANCE IS NEEDED URGENTLY !!!!!!
To: "Eloy Savimbi" <e_savimbi456@yahoo.co.uk>

Dear Elroy:

Sorry to make you wait for my response! I just got home from
the hospital, where I had surgery to remove an embryonic
conjoined twin from my backside. I feel so free without little
"Edna" clinging to my rear and forcing me to wear baggy
pants. And waking me up with her barking.

I am so sorry to hear about your father. I lost my own dad
year before last when he was accidentally loaded into a silo
along with the cattle feed.

We did not know what went with him until a farmhand found a
wristwatch in a pile of manure. By that time, the cattle were
nearly ready to send to market, so my brother and I decided
the best thing was to let them finish the remaining silage. I
regret the decision, as now I burst into tears every time I pass
a McDonald's.

I hope you will see fit to let me in on this deal. I could use the
cash. Edna was hardly what you would call "a person," but I
would still like to buy her a plot with a nice monument.

Stephanie Hopkins
Golgi Apparatus, UT

I knew I was swinging for the bleachers with that one,
and Elroy turned out to be unusually bright for a spammer,
because he sent me this:

Date: Wed, 14 Sep 2005 10:26:01 +0100 (BST)
From: "Eloy Savimbi"<e_savimbi456@yahoo.co.uk>

Subject: Re: YOUR ASSISTANCE IS NEEDED URGENTLY!!!!!!
To: "Stephanie Hopkins"

Dear,

Thanks for your stories, i will wnt you to help me in this
business if really you want to send to me your phone numbers
and contact detials and your id card asap.

Then i will give you the security company contact number.

savimbi jr.

Edna never got her tombstone, but Stephie gave an orderly
five bucks to put a pink bow on the medical waste bag.

I got an interesting e-mail, from a person calling himself
Dakarai Gamba. Mr. Gamba was concerned that I might be
disturbed by the unexpected communication. I have to show
you most of the e-mail, because I refer back to it in my
response.

Date: Mon, 15 Aug 2005 14:21:40 +0200
From: gamdak@dirtbag.com
Subject: Hello Friend!!!

Dear Friend,

This might seem very deplorable for a person that you do
not know, I got your contact from the Belgian chamber of
commece and decided to contact you for an important
assistance. I am Dakarai Gamba a citizen of Zimbabwe, but
I am writing from my refugee camp in Belgium.

I am the only son of Dakarai Banga, a wealthy farmer and a
senior politician with the opposition political party in my

country, Movement for Democratic Change [MDC]. My father was murdered by our wicked President, Robert Mugabe and I fled my country because I have become his next target to eliminate.

My father was a fighter for Justice and a moving force in the MDC, a party wanting to end the several years of brutal dictatorship government of President Robert Mugabe. My father was accused of Treason and also assisting the White farmers in fighting the government.

[SNIP]

My father kept this money in a trunk box in disguise as family treasures and could not bank them, because of the situation in my country. My father's business, farms and banks account were seized by the government before hisfarrest and murder. He told me everything concerning the funds while he wasfstill in detention.

[SNIP]

Thank you and God bless.

Sincerely Yours.
Dakarai Gamba.
(For the family)

What IS it with that "for the family" stuff? They say that over and over. Do they sit around over there watching *The Sopranos* on pirate satellite dishes? And what kind of nut calls an unwanted e-mail "deplorable"? "Annoying," maybe. "Silly." "Stupid." But "deplorable"? "Deplorably stupid" would be better.

However, Steve Hopkins strongly agreed. And he thought Dakarai's dad was kind of a Tom.

Date: Thu, 8 Sep 2005 13:44:37 -0700 (PDT)
From: "Steve H."
Subject: Re: Dear Friend
To: gamdak@dirtbag.com

Well, it certainly is deplorable, writing a person you don't even know. My humiliation and disturbment are pretty severe. But it looks like there is a buck to be made here, so forget all that.

I am not surprised to learn that your dad was killed by the President. We have a President here who kills people right and left. He killed a bunch of people in Afghanistan, and he killed a bunch of people in Iraq, and he kills us by putting arsenic in our water, and he killed a whole slew of Americans by refusing to sign a Japanese treaty that would have made the hurricanes go away. He is not going to be satisfied until we are all dead, and he is so damn dumb he is not even going to tax our estates.

I'm sorry to hear that your dad helped the white people, because they cause problems wherever they go, and if folks in Zambibwia were killing them, they probably had a damn good reason. I myself am a Native American (1/32nd on my stepmother's side), and if it weren't for those white son of a bitches, I would probably own a whole slew of casinos today instead of working for the highway department, running a gang vibrator.

I consulted a tribal elder I met at a pancake house, and he told me my spirit guide was the great spotted tit. I was hoping for something cool, like the polar bear, but apparently the good ones are all taken.

I haven't actually seen the tit. It's my understanding that you have to spend a day in a sweat lodge and smoke a considerable amount of weed.

I have to say that I am shocked that they put your father in detention before they murdered him. I hope they didn't make him clap erasers.

I'm ready to move on this thing whenever you are.

Steve Hopkins
Elk Tonsil, MT
(For the Tribe)

I know you'll think I'm lying, but Daiquiri or Daktari or whatever his name was got back to me after that and thanked me profusely for my response. But I had so many other spammers to keep track of, I simply forgot to keep playing him.

There really is a road-building machine called a gang vibrator.

I'll give you one more short example before moving on to heavier matters. This one didn't get a response, but I'm so proud of it, I'm going to show it to you anyway. I don't know why spammers think they can use the name of Allah to get in good with Americans, who are currently scrambling to prevent the Muslim faithful from detonating nuclear weapons in America's major cities, but they invoke his name quite often.

From: Mrs Aisha Mohammed:

SALAMALEKUM,
! Greetings in the name of Allah, the most beneficent, the most merciful.

My name is Mrs Aishat Abdulahi Mohameed, a widow to Late
Mr A, Mohammed

I am 74 years old, Presently I am suffering from long time
cancer of the breast, from all indications, my condition is really
deteriorating and i am very much afraid of my dorctor's report,
infact my condition is very bad now, My late husband was
killed during the Gulf war, and during the period of our
marriage we couldn't produce any child . . .

So now i have decided to divide part of this wealth, to
contribute to the propagation of Islam and in assisting the less-
privileged Muslim faithful and all humanity in Africa and
thruoghout the Muslim world, I chossed you . . .

Yours in Allah,
Mrs Aishat Mohamed.
aishadurkadurkamohammed@jihad.com

Steve Hopkins may be a lot of things, but he is no Muslim.
Pray along with him and join his exciting new faith.

Dear Mrs. Mohameed:

First of all, let me tell you how sorry I am to hear about your
medical condition and the loss of your husband. My heart
goes out to you.

I must tell you, I am quite interested in your proposition.
However, there is one small snag.

I cannot help deducing that you are a Muslim. Unfortunately,
my conscience will not permit me to become a business
partner with a person who worships an imaginary god who
will not let his worshipers use toilet paper. But because your

letter is so tempting, I would like to see if we can work
something out.

You see, I would like to tell you about my faith. I am a Moorist.
I worship the large American journalist Michael Moore.

Every morning, I say the following prayer while anointing
myself with the drippings from a bucket of Kentucky Fried
Chicken:

Oh Moore, bless thy folds, wherein is stored thy bounty.

Bless thy chins and wattles and let me nest therein.

*Bless thy vast and cavernous pants, within which the
faithful and their vehicles may take refuge.*

*Bless the fermented sweat of thy corpulent body, which
ever reeks in the nostrils of the chosen. May it ever evade
the wickedness of those who would remove it with a
shower brush or perhaps a fire hose.*

*Bless thy lies and fantasies, which ever pass like flatus from
the unshorn crevice which is thought by scientists to be thy
mouth.*

*Oh Moore, bless thy buttocks. May they never become a
portion for mongooses.*

*This day shall I sate myself on Zingers, vomit, and then sate
myself again, that I may remake myself in thy creased and
dimpled image. The soap shall I shun, and also the razor.*

*The crumbs shall I roll in. The wrappers shall I paste to the
tips of my pendulous man-boobs.*

Grant me the power to lie as thou doest, to leftist acclaim.

Surely book deals and movies shall follow me to the end of my days.

Amen.

So anyway, Mrs. Mohameed, if you would be so good as to remove your clothes, anoint yourself with shortening, and publicly renounce your alliance with this nonexistent "Allah" person, and then if you will please recite the above prayer while chewing Oreos with your mouth open, I think we can do business.

Steve "Son of Moore" Hopkins
Weenusburg, NH

That must have freaked her out pretty good. I don't know if she converted or not. But now when she faces the Almighty Moore on the day of judgment, and she can't produce a ticket stub from *Bowling for Columbine,* she can't say she wasn't warned.

Okay, that's enough of the short exchanges for now, Moore be praised. On to bigger projects.

Stephie's mind was wont to wander as Consuelo's skillful fingers worked the bones and muscles of her tired back. She lay prostrate on the massage table, determinedly gripping the straw that ran from the mai tai up to her face. It had been frustrating, trying to make Consuelo understand the word "subluxation." She never did get a handle on it. But she acquitted herself admirably for an ignorant foreigner who had to be reminded over and over not to use the toilet brush on the kitchen sink.

Stephie closed her eyes, causing flakes of bright blue eye shadow to flitter down into her drink. She tried to conjure Mr. Savimbi's face and his broad, powerful shoulders. Would Lawrence ever forgive her? Certainly, he would.

After all, it was he, not she, who had had the fateful rendezvous with the diaper truck.

Early on, I decided I didn't want to give these morons my real name. My e-mail account had the name "Steve H." associated with it, so I decided to use that as a basis for a new identity. That was how I came to create Stephanie Hopkins, the randy dowager of Buttville, Nevada, and other locations I make up on the fly.

Stephanie is a Protean character. Her health, personal history, hometown, and financial status vary depending on what I want the 419er to know. Don't obsess on consistency. Tormenting spammers is an art, so facts take a backseat to artistic considerations. Mostly I worry about what will make the spammer look most ridiculous. Also, I have a terrible memory, so I couldn't be consistent if I tried.

Stephanie has a lovely passport photo that I created myself. It's a lot like the Al Franken passports I send out when I use a male alias. I took a headshot of sexy octogenarian journalist Helen Thomas and superimposed it on a real passport. Then I rearranged the lettering so the passport bore Stephie's name. Whenever Stephie starts a new correspondence, she makes sure that passport photo goes out right away. They fall for it every time. No one has ever written back and said, "Dude, that's Helen Thomas."

Stephanie made her debut in an e-mail to one Robertson Savimbi. A relative of Elroy's, I guess. I lost a bunch of the e-mail headers, but I kept the meat. Here is Robertson's first e-mail to Stephanie.

From: "ROBERTSON SAVIMBI"
Reply-To: savimbi_robertson007@squalor.net
Date: Thu Jan 30 00:11:36 2003
Subject: PLEASE ASSIST ME

Dear friend,

I am sincerely seeking for your urgent help in respect to safe keeping of some of my Uncle's money that arose from Diamonds sales. This money (US$18.5million) . . .

For your reliable assistance, I will reward you with 15% of the money . . .

Sincerely,

R.Savimbi

Wow! That's a lot of money! Stephanie's arthritic fingers trembled as she typed her response.

Dear Mrs. Savimbi:

My stars and buttons, I can't believe my good luck! Can it really be true? Of COURSE I will help you!

I called my bank because I was afraid they would have trouble putting that much money in my savings account, because it already has $620,000 in it. But they said to go right ahead.

Please get back to me as soon as possible. I'm supposed to leave for Lake Havasu with my friend Mabel day after tomorrow, but I guess that can wait if it has to.

Mrs. Stephanie Hopkins
Coral Springs, Florida

Stephanie frequently makes errors of spelling and gender. "Senior moments," I guess.
Savimbi got back to her.

THANK YOU VERY MUCH FOR YOUR ANTICIPATED ASSISTANCE . . .

THE SECURITY COMPANY IS BASED IN HOLLAND. YOU WILL BE REQUIRED TO TRAVEL TO HOLLAND TO CLEAR AND RECEIVE THE CONSIGNMENT . . .

BASED ON MY PRESENT CONDITION, I AM FINACIALLY NOT CAPABLE TO PAY FOR MORE CHARGES THAT MAY ACCRUE WITH TIME. SO IN THIS RESPECT, I WILL APPRECIATE IF YOU CAN BE VERY TIMEOUS IN MAKING ME KNOW YOUR POSITION ON WHETHER YOU CAN HANDLE THIS TRANSACTION OR NOT . . . BOTH YOUR TELEPHONE AND FAX NUMBERS IS REQUIRED SO THAT I CAN TALK TO YOU VIA PHONE . . .

AND MY CELL # IS 447753262320.

Oh my! Holland! The place they named the tunnel for! She wrote back immediately. She was nothing if not "TIMEOUS."

Dear Mrs. Savimbi:

I'm answering your e-mail immediately! I hope that's timeous enough for you!

Holland! How exciting! I can't believe this is happening to me! I've always wanted to see the fjords!

I'm shaking as I write this! Although that could partly be my thyroid.

I will be available all weekend, except Saturday afternoon, when I play mah jongg at the community center. You may call me at 305-944-xxxx [Miami FBI branch office] or fax me at my brother-in-law's, at 305-448-xxxx. [Kinko's Copy Center fax line]

Since we are being confidential, please do not tell anyone I have over $600,000 in my bank account. My late husband hid a lot of cash from the government, and my children don't even know. I make them pay for my gas!

By the way, I saw your Mr. Mandela on TV yesterday, and I have to say, he's a marvelous man. I love those colorful shirts. Perhaps one day you could send me one.

Mrs. Stephanie Hopkins
Coral Springs, Florida

There are one-celled animals living in pond water that would realize this was a bogus e-mail, but Mrs. Savimbi the

Nigerian 419 transsexual did not get the picture. Back he came for more. How many times did I tell him my name was Stephanie? Still he called me Steve. Stephanie is not the only one with gender-identification problems.

Subject: EXPECT MY CALL TOMORROW.

HELLO STEVE, GOT YOUR MAIL TODAY, BE ASSURED OF MY SECRECY IN TRANSACTING THIS PROJECT. I WILL DEFINATILY CALL YOU TOMORROW SO THAT I CAN GIVE YOU THE FULL DETAILS REQURIED IN CARRYING OUT THIS TRANSACTION.

I CANT WAIT FOR THIS FUNDS TO BE CLEARED SO THAT WE CAN SIT TOGETHER AND DISSCUSS INVESTMENT MODALITIES.

ALL I NEED FROM YOU AT THIS STAGE IS MAXIMUM TRUST AND UTMOST SECRECY.

MY REGARDS,
R.SAVIMBI.

Now, I hope you will forgive me for this. But I decided to test Savimbi's greed. I decided to make it plain that, though warmhearted and sincere, Stephie was about as socially enlightened as George Wallace.

Dear Mrs. Savimbi:

I look forward to hearing from you! I'm so excited! I spent two hours yesterday looking at Winnebagos! My Lawrence always wanted to get one and tour the scenic Wisconsin cheese country, but two weeks after he retired, he stepped off a curb and was crushed by a diaper truck. Now I'll have to take my friend Mabel, although she is sadly lactose intolerant.

I will try to answer the phone personally, although I don't always make it to the phone first now that I have two carbon-fiber hips. In the event Consuelo answers, I will take the phone from her as quickly as possible. I am very, very embarrassed to admit this, but if she hears your accent, she may be short with you. I'm sorry to say she has a thing about Negroes. Please, please don't hold it against me! She is just an ignorant foreigner.

In her defense, she is clean and honest and makes hospital corners. I feel sorry for her because she is illiterate and superstitious. Last year I bought her two gold teeth.

I am not like Consuelo! I am a tremendous fan of Xavier Cugat, who is practically black, and I voted for David Duke in the last presidential primary. In case you don't know, he is a famous colored politician.

Mrs. Stephanie Hopkins
Coral Springs, Florida

All right, all right! I am a bad person. I should not have written that. Of course, if Chris Rock had written it, you'd say it was genius. Fine, I'll send a hundred bucks to the NAACP. Grow up and get over it.

I pushed Mrs. Savimbi a tiny bit too far, so I never heard from him again. But the great thing about 419 spammers is that as soon as you get rid of one, another one pops up in his place. Always remember, my friends, as I once told one of my accidental pen pals: Nigerians are 100 percent fungible.

******************Midgets, Edible Lingerie,****************** a Paper Gown, and Crown Royal**

It was a slow night at the Golden Heifer. Chester stood by the stage as the girls waddled out and began intertwining their ponderous limbs with the specially reinforced poles. He didn't anticipate any problems from the customers. Drink sales were never good in strip joints that attracted mostly Muslims.

A few feet away, Rhonda turned her back to the crowd and began to booty-clap. Tiny hairs on Chester's neck registered the impact of shock waves emanating from her quivering backside.

Suddenly she misplaced a foot and squealed in surprise, and then everything was dark. No light. No sound. No sensation.

Only the curiously comforting scent of lukewarm Jägermeister.

It was gradually becoming apparent to me that African spammers know about as much about life in America as a goose knows about Christmas. I can understand that. After I saw *Crouching Tiger, Hidden Dragon,* I spent the better part of a month convinced that Chinese people could fly.

As I came to comprehend the depth and breadth of their ignorance, I became more and more cavalier about what I told the spammers.

Let me introduce Richard Dewar, a man I later defamed with such ruthlessness I scared even myself.

From: RICHARD DEWAR [mailto:richdewar90210@asshead.az]
Sent: Sunday, May 09, 2004 11:27 AM
Subject: GREETINGS FROM SOUTH AFRICA

Greetings

How are you and your family I hope that you are all okay? I want to ask you, If you are not capable to quietly look for a reliable and honest person who will be capable and fit to provide either an existing bank account or to set up a new Bank a/c immediately to receive this money, even an empty a/c can serve to receive this money, as long as you will remain honest to me till the end for this important business trusting in you and believing in God that you will never let me down either now or in future . . .

The total amount involve is Eighteen million Six Hundred Thousand United States Dollars only [$18,600,000.00] and we wish to transfer this money into a safe foreigners account abroad. But I don't know any foreigner, I am only contacting you as a foreigner because this money can not be approved to a local person here, but to a foreigner who has information about the account, which I shall give to you upon your positive response . . .

I decided it was time for Stephanie to have a son. His name is Chester. Well, it WAS Chester. Before the rogue hamster got him.

Date: Sun, 9 May 2004 10:03:30 -0700 (PDT)
From: "Steve H."
Subject: Re: FW: GREETINGS FROM SOUTH AFRICA
To: richdewar90210@asshead.az

Dear Mr. Dewar:

Thank you for your exciting e-mail!

As to your first inquiry, I must sadly state that no, my family is not okay. My son Chester recently passed away due to a freak accident in which a hamster chewed a hole in his ventilator bag. Chester was a paraplegic due to injuries received at his job. He was an emcee at a gentlemen's club featuring what are known as "BBWs" and one of the girls slipped on some spilled Jagermeester and fell off the stage, crushing several of his vertebrae and rupturing his anus, if you can imagine such a thing.

I am writing from Chester's e-mail address, where he received your message. Apparently he used this address to correspond with a number of women currently housed in corrective facilities, so I had to check his e-mail and tell them to stop sending photos and that they would not be receiving any more funds via PayPal.

I do not know if you have Jagermeester over there. I hope I am spelling it right.

I knew better than to let him give little Rex the run of the bed, but he and Chester were quite attached to each other. Of course, I was quite furious when I found Rex nibbling on the deflated bag. He has since been flushed.

I still have a lot of medical bills to pay, as well as a fine for animal cruelty, so your amazing e-mail comes as great news. Of COURSE I will help. I hope I am eligible to participate; your e-mail calls for a "safe foreigner," but I have lived here in the United States my entire life. My maid Consuelo is a foreigner; I suppose we can use her if needed. Her immigration status is iffy, so she has to do whatever I tell her.

I would like to put this money in my Schwab account. It already contains over $350,000 US, but I have been assured that there is no limit to what I can deposit. I guess I can give you the account number and the authority to make transactions.

PLEASE CONTACT ME AS SOON AS POSSIBLE! My telephone number is 202-xxx-xxxx [John Kerry Campaign, national headquarters].

Tuesdays are no good; that's mah jonng day.

Stephanie Hopkins
Coral Springs, FL

It's embarrassing that Stephie misspelled "mah jongg," but on the day she typed that e-mail, she was hitting the Bacardi pretty good.

I didn't hear back from Mr. Dewar. But I mention him anyway because of the part he played in a series of e-mails later that year. It's not actually true to say he played a part. Yes, his name appeared on the e-mails. But he isn't the person who wrote them.

The story of Mr. Dewar's unwitting participation in the abuse of a fellow African begins with a message Stephanie Hopkins received from a gentleman named Olademeji Afolabi. Sorry about the missing headers.

From: bizman@malaria.it:
Hello,

I am the son of an immediate past Minister of an African country who was removed from office because of an aledged US$214million when he was a member of the national identity card scheme in that country . . .

*Time is of great essence in this matter so if I do not hear from
your within the next three days I will take it that you are not
interested and will solicit for a new partner.*
Waiting to hear from you.
Olademeji Afolabi

A deadline! Oh my God! Stephie had to jump on this juicy
deal RIGHT AWAY! She wanted to open a business, and she
just had to tell Afolabi all about it.

Date: Wed, 12 May 2004 09:42:45 -0700 (PDT)
From: "Steve H."
Subject: Re: CONTACT ME IMMEDIATELY.
To: bizman@malaria.it

Dear Mr. or Mrs. Afolabi:

Land sakes! I never dreamed a total stranger would offer me
an opportunity like this! Of course, I am highly interested. I am
a widow on a fixed income, so the chance to make this kind
of scratch is most welcome.

As luck would have it, I have a marvelous investment idea, but
until now, I never thought it would become a reality. Keep this
under your hat. I know what interesting hats you people have
over there. I came up with it during a shuffleboard game with
my friend Mabel from the Senior Center. We want to open
Nevada's first drive-thru brothel for seniors.

Here's how we figure. Older men have the same urges as the
rest of us, but due to problems with their hips and knees, they
are not always up to the long walk from the car. And if they
fall and break something, there are liability issues, and it gets
the police and EMTs involved, because you can't just leave

them lying on the sidewalk. So our plan is to buy a Sonic drive-in that went out of business and send ladies out to the customers. And since much of the equipment would still be in place, we would also be in a position to offer treats such as foot-longs and cheese tots. Mabel and I figure we need about two hundred grand in order to get the business going and make our nut while we build a client base.

By the way, this is totally legal in Nevada. As long as we don't do anything really weird. You know. Sheep and chickens and such. Of course, I am not being judgemental. I know that kind of activity is more accepted in Nigeria.

Give me your contact info, and we'll get started. I can't wait to tell the girls at the Senior Center.

Stephanie Hopkins
Buttville, NV

The most improbable bit here is the sentence about the Sonic drive-in going out of business. Have you ever eaten at Sonic? Oh my God. It hurts to think about it. Foot-long hot dogs with chili and cheese and slaw. Huge piles of cheese tots. Sugary, slushy drinks big enough to chill champagne in. If I get rich from this book, I'm going to buy a house next to one.

I figured this was another throwaway. No one could be stupid enough to respond to a story like that.

No one but Afolabi.

Dear Stephanie Hopkins,

Thank you for your response. I have spent so much energy, money and time in getting This particular business deal to this stage. I want Somebody like you who really wants to achieve success To form an association that will be awe-inspiring, so That we take immediate possession of this money . . .

Do you have an international passport? Please, I would Need
your full names as written in your international Passport . . .

Will you be there for me? Are you sure you can be Trusted?
Or, do we sign an agreement, scan it and send To each other
after both of us must have signed? Or, Do we just transact in
good faith and trust each Other? Please, pardon my
skepticism. You know I have To make sure my brother's,
finances are properly kept, And I would not want any
disappointment . . .

p.s: I am happy to help in your investment and willing to
support.

It can be disarming when a Nigerian turns out to be that
stupid. It's hard to decide what to do. I decided Stephanie's
libido should come into play.

Dear Mr. Afolabi:

**My, that was quick. I did not expect you to be so efficient! If
all Nigerians are this businesslike, I have to wonder why
Nigeria is such a squalid and miserable place!**

**I am not sure what an international passport is. I have a
regular U.S. passport, which I used when I went to Lourdes to
soak my prolapse and pray for healing. But you probably don't
want to hear about my medical problems. It didn't work, so I
think laser surgery is going to be unavoidable. I can't believe I
live in a day and age when a doctor will actually shoot a laser
beam up a person's rear end. It's like being on *Star Trek,* only
I'm wearing a paper gown and out of my mind on Valium and
Crown Royal.**

**My name on my passport is Stephanie Himmler Hopkins. The
Himmler comes from my mother's people. They immigrated**

from Germany in the fifties because their neighbors kept painting filthy slogans on the side of their Mercedes and filling their mailbox with manure.

Will I be there for you? I'm not sure how you mean that. If you mean am I trustworthy, why of course I am. I admit, a few years back, I passed a bad check to a Jehovah's Witness, but that was only because he made it to the door before I could turn on the sprinklers.

If you mean something else, all I can say is, with all the replacement hormones I'm taking, you probably could not keep up with me. I'm not making any promises, but please send a photo. If you're not shy, shirtless is fine.

I am thrilled that you want to invest in the brothel. As luck would have it, one of my mah jongg buddies is the widow of a gentleman who owned a supply house that catered to the trade, and she has kept the business going, so we ought to be able to save a lot of money on—excuse the frank language—items such as French ticklers and vibrating [name of disgusting sexual appliance omitted] that work off a cigarette lighter.

I await your instructions.

Stephanie Hopkins
Buttville, NV

Now, TELL me you know someone stupid enough to follow up on an e-mail like that. Try and conceive of stupidity that profound. It could never happen. It's like a bad *Kids in the Hall* sketch. Or is it?

Dear Steve H,

I have received your e-mail. And all is well understood my Good friend. I thank you for assisting us in this transaction. I also want to assure you that everything has been perfected with my position. I also want you to understand that you have nothing to bother about. Congratulations, these funds have been transferred from The Netherlands to The United Kingdom for security reasons. I will let you inform you of the bank in uk by saturday. I will also need your phone or fax numbers so that i can reach you asap.

Okay, he is still on the hook, AND he thinks Stephanie's name is Steve. He's not the brightest candle on the Kwanzaa menorah. Stephie decided to crank the throttle just a bit.

WOW!!!

I can't believe this is happening!

By the way, "Steve" is my son Chester's middle name, which is why it appears on my e-mails. I assure you, I am very much female. VERY much. Do you understand? *grin* Although last year I did have a hysterectomy scare.

You never did send that photo.

My private phone number is 305-685-7xxx [Club Rolex, a ghetto strip joint famous for bottle tricks]. **I also got a toll-free line so I could take calls from my grandkids, Belinda and Mee Nob Lo. Mee Nob's daddy is Thai, in case you're wondering.**

My fax number is 305-856-9xxx [French Consulate, Miami]. **Please write "MONSIEUR CHIRAC MANGEMERDE" at the top. Mr. Mangemerde is my housekeeper.**

I can't wait to hear your voice! God bless!

Stephanie Hopkins
Buttville, NV

OOPS

Dear Olademeji:

Silly me! I forgot to include my toll-free number! It's 1-866-303-2xxx [offices of Air America Radio]. Call any time, night or day.

Your Stephie

Okay, you have to pay close attention now. Remember Richard Dewar, the spammer from South Africa? Stephie did. And she thought it would be interesting if he contacted her and gave his opinion of Afolabi. So I created an address for Richard Dewar and used it to send Stephie an e-mail, which I then forwarded to Afolabi.

Are you with me here? Richard Dewar is me. Stephie is me. Afolabi is a for-real Nigerian imbecile.

Dear Olademeji:

I think you should know, I received an e-mail from another gentleman in Africa, and I mentioned you to him! Look what he says about you!

I really don't know what to think. By the way, he is offering substantially more money than you are!

From: "RICHARD DEWAR"
Subject: GREETINGS FROM SOUTH AFRICA
Date: Fri, 14 May 2004 11:27:29 -0400

Dearest Stephanie:

Greetings

How are you and your family I hope that you are all okay? I am in receipt of your fine e-mail regarding your contact with the fellow from Nigeria.

With greatest sadness, I must inform you that this man is a bloody scoundrel, and that you must immediately cease from all contacts with him! I know this Afolabi well. His father is highly notorious here in Africa for committing the most indecent type of assaults on young boys, and his mother is a common prostitute! He himself was once jailed—I am ashamed to say this to a proper integritable lady such as yourself—for abnormal relations with an unconscious person at the scene of a bus crash.

It is very clear to me that this unreliable and dishonest fellow wishes to take you into his confidence and then abscond with your funds. If I were in Nigeria, I would seek him out and whip him like a dog.

Please ignore his emails, and I will alert the proper authorities to his activities.

I hope you liked my photo. It is most unusual for a business associate to request a picture of me in a bathing costume, but I was glad to pose for you.

I have contacted your bank and confirmed the information you provided, and I shall endeavour to make the deposit before the month is out.

Trusting in God, your obdt. svt.,
Richard

WAIT! It gets better. I also sent an e-mail directly to Afolabi from Dewar's address. Remember, now, I'm pretending
to be Richard Dewar, and Afolabi is a real person. And naturally, I forwarded all this crap to the real Richard Dewar.
For the hell of it.

DEAR SIR

IT IS MY MOST UNFORTUNATE UNDERSTANDING THAT YOU
HAVE BEEN CORRESPONDING WITH ONE MRS S HOPKINS
OF BUTTVILLE, NEVADA, IN THE HOPES OF PERSUADING
HER TO PROVIDE YOU WITH BANK INFORMATION

MRS HOPKINS PROVIDED ME WITH YOUR EMAIL ADDRESS
AND I MUST INSIST THAT YOU DESIST ALL
COMMUNICATIONS WITH HER

I HAVE BEEN WORKING ON MRS HOPKINS FOR OVER
THREE WEEKS AND I AM AWAITING A LETTER IN WHICH
SHE WILL PROVIDE ME WITH HER BANK INFORMATION. I
HAVE PUT A GOOD DEAL OF LABOUR INTO THIS AND I
SHALL NOT STAND FOR YOUR INTERFERENCE

I HAVE GONE SO FAR AS TO SEND THE WOMAN
PHOTOGRAPHS OF MY NEPHEW OKEFENOKI IN A BATHING
COSTUME STATING THAT HE IS I. I HAVE NOT COME THIS
FAR TO LOSE OUT TO AN IGNORANT NIGERIAN

FIND YOURSELF A NEW AMERICAN CONTACT OR I AND MY
BOYS WILL COME TO YOUR COUNTRY AND TAKE CARE OF
YOU, YOU INSOLENT AND UNRELIABLE MAN

IF YOU WILL PROVIDE A POSTAL ADDRESS I AM WILLING
TO SEND YOU 500 USD ONCE MRS HOPKINS' CAPITAL IS IN

**HAND, IF YOU WILL JUST DROP THIS MATTER AND NOT
RUIN IT FOR ME**

**RICHARD DEWAR
JOHANNESBURG**

Afolabi did not like that one bit. He was hopping mad.
He sent the following response to Stephie:

Dear Stephanie,

I hoped that i could say Good morning but i am too
disappointed to say it. I thought we had an understanding
about my family and how confidential the issue was. I was
really hoping and still do hope that we can commence and
conclude this project but i dont trust you. I received a mail
from a Richard this morning totally insulting me and accusing
me of everything wrong. He now threatened my life and that
of my family if i dont break communication with you. I dont
know what you expect of me or you still dont believe me. If
we are going to commence this project we have to trust each
other. I will have to tell you that what ever you have with the
him isn't any of my concern. So please dont allow what we
are trying to build here be crumbled by a foreigner. I will
expect your mail. Expect my international passport by later
Today.

Take care,

Olademeji Afolabi.

He also gave Richard Dewar a piece of his tiny mind, with
which he could ill afford to part:

Dear Sir,

I am very tensed and shocked by your outburst. For the reason be i dont know you and have anything doing with You. So i dont know why you are angry with me. I am trying to help my family here and you are insulting me. Please i dont have time for games and dont have time to argue but i will warn you that i dont like being threatened, so please behave like a matured man and I dont need your money. Be civilised.

Olademeji Afolabi.

Stephie was very contrite. She got back to Afolabi and apologized and tried to get the deal back on track. After all, that drive-in brothel wasn't going to finance itself. She also tried to squeeze some cash out of him for charity.

Dear Olademeji:

I feel just terrible. I should have kept your information confidential, but I was so confused. I am just a poor widow with dreams of opening an erotic drive-in, and here I was, suddenly dealing with two foreign gentlemen offering to make me rich . . . I tell you, compared to this, hot flashes are a walk in the park.

I will not communicate further with Mr. Dewar. He told me some sob story about his father needing an operation for a revolting disease, and he admitted the photos he sent were of another person, so I turned him in to the South African authorities.

Before we go any further, I think you should send me a small token to confirm your good faith and prove you're really there in Nigeria. For all I know, you could be a frat boy in Wisconsin, pulling my leg in order to get money for beer and XTC. I would appreciate it if you would forward fifteen US dollars to me via my friend Susan Army at S. [as in "Salvation"] Army, 2900 Palomino Lane, Las Vegas NV 89107. Cash is fine.

Stephie

It occurred to me that threatening to beat the crap out of a spammer might be some sort of federal crime, so Richard Dewar had a change of heart, too:

MR AFOLABI:

I MUST APOLOGZIE FOR MY UNFORTUNATE BEHAVIOR. IT IS AN EMBARRASSMENT FOR A PART-TIME CLERGYMAN SUCH AS MYSELF TO ADMIT IT, BUT I WAS QUITE INEBRIATED WHEN I EMAILED YOU EARLIER, AND MY REMARKS WERE QUITE BEYOND THE PALE. PLEASE FORGIVE ME AND HAVE NO WORRIES FOR YOUR SECURITY.

I TRULY BELIEVED MRS. HOPKINS HAD THE POTENTIAL TO ASSIST ME WITH MY FINANCIAL DIFFICULTIES BUT SUCH IS NOT THE CASE. THIS SCHEMING FEMALE TRICKED ME INTO SENDING HER FIFTEEN USD AS PROOF OF MY EXISTENCE AND GOOD FAITH, AND SHE REPAID MY TRUST BY REPORTING ME TO THE AUTHORITIES, TO WHOM I SPENT THE BETTER PART OF THE MORNING DENYING ALL KNOWLEDGE OF HER.

PLEASE UNDERSTAND I DO NOT POSSESS THE INCLINATION FOR VIOLENCE. I AM A SIMPLE MANICURIST HERE IN JOHANNESBURG AND RATHER SLIGHT. I WAS MERELY ATTEMPTING TO ACCUMULATE FUNDS FOR SURGERY TO REVERSE MY FATHER'S TERRIBLE CASE OF

GYNECOMASTIA, AND IT LOOKED AS THOUGH YOU WERE
GOING TO BOLLOCKS THE WHOLE EFFORT.

NOW IT APPEARS PAPA WILL CONTINUE HAVING TO WEAR
LOOSE SHIRTS A WHILE LONGER, WHILE I RESOLVE MY
DIFFICULTIES WITH THE LAW. ON THE UP SIDE, HE HAS
HAD SEVERAL OFFERS FOR JOBS AS AN EXOTIC DANCER.

I WILL NOT CONTACT YOU AGAIN. BE WARY OF THIS
DECEITFUL WOMAN, AND IF YOU ARE EVER IN
JOHANNESBURG, LOOK ME UP SO I CAN MAKE AMENDS
VIA A HUMBLE DINNER AND A FREE MANICURE.

RICHARD DEWAR

I have to wonder what Richard Dewar thought when he
received that e-mail, ostensibly from himself.

Afolabi is a forgiving sort, so he decided to put the unfortunate Dewar business behind him and get on with scam-
ming Stephanie.

Dear Stephanie,

Morning To You. I have received Your email and all is well
understood. I want to let you know that this funds have been
transferred to United kingdom so you have to prepare yourself
to clear this funds from United Kingdom. I want to know if the
bank has contacted you for the immediate transfer of the
funds. I will like you to disregard any illegal Group of people
here in My country because there is a lot of scam all over the
world including My country to avoid misconduct. Please
update me if the bank has contacted you:

My Good Friend, i am sending my international passport. For
You To know that you are dealing with the right person. I
want you to call me as soos as you receive this message

through my telephone number 234 8037183508, CALL ME
FOR MORE ADVICE.

Nice speaking with you and Blessings.

Afolabi Olatunde Olademeji.

He's like a dog that keeps coming back no matter how
hard you kick it.

Is his name really Olademeji Afolabi (or vice versa)? I
don't know. But here is his passport, so you won't think I
pull all this stuff out of my rear end.

Stephie was enchanted by Afolabi's steely gaze, firm jaw,
and remarkable resemblance to actor Lou Gossett, Jr. She
sent him a nice response, which included a scan of her own
passport.

Dear Afolabi:

I am so sorry I did not get back to you. My friend Mabel had a
birthday last week, and we took her to a strip show in Reno—
it's quite fascinating; the performers are all midgets—and
while walking to the stage to be an audience participant, I

stepped in Mabel's spilled banana banshee, fell, and cracked my head on the edge of a table.

Do not worry; I was in the hospital for a day, and since then I have had some problems with double vision and mild incontinence, but I am told it will blow over in a couple of weeks.

I am attaching a scan of my own passport. I hope you like it. I'm not exactly sure what you intend to do with it, but I trust you implicitly.

I don't suppose you have any photos of you that show more than just your handsome face?

Your Stephie

In order to avoid being sued by Helen Thomas, and for the protection of the reading public, I have removed the photo.

A midget strip club. This is how far I went to get rid of Olademeji Afolabi. I don't know what else I could have said, short of claiming Stephanie lived on the moon and commuted to earth on a magic sleigh pulled by pixies. But here is his next e-mail. He still can't absorb the fact that my name is Stephanie:

Dear Steve,

Good Morning? How was your day? I am sorry to hear about the accident and i hope you are recovering swiftly. I have also received your international passport, you must understand that this is only for identification purposes and nothing else Because i need to know who i am entrusting these funds to. I also want to know if you have contacted the bank (STANDARD FINANCIAL TRUST). It is important you do so. I remember i sent you a mail with there information. You can contact the Head of Operations there Mr Ric Castillo for details. His Telephone number is +442070600273. Once you do this i need you to call me because if we are to aquire these funds we need to be communicating frequently. You should have my number by now so feel free to call me.

It is really good hearing from you and i know we shall accomplish greatness in the weeks to come. Call The bank immediately to know how you will collect the money.

Take care,

Olademeji Afolabi.

Oh God. When would he get a clue? I was starting to dread his e-mails.

Dear Olademeji:

Thank you so much for your get-well e-mail. I am feeling somewhat better. The double vision is gone, and I think the incontinence is over. Until I am sure, I am staying off of the carpet.

I had a dizzy spell yesterday while belly dancing at the senior center, so unfortunately today I am in the hospital for tests. It has been a trying stay. This morning I was given three barium enemas in a row. I kept telling them the injury was at my other end, and finally they realized there was a problem with the nursing station computer. If you think I didn't give them a piece of my mind, when I finally got out of the bathroom, you have another think coming.

This afternoon, several dancers from the midget strip show came by to wish me well and sing me a song. I was very touched. It was hard to see them clearly, with them on the floor and me in the bed with two fused vertebrae in my neck. But I could hear them very well when they sang the popular song "Short, Short Man" in three-part harmony.

I will have limited ability to check my e-mail for the next day or two, but I will be home soon and we can resume our delightful correspondence. I really do wish you would send a better photo.

Your Stephie
Buttville, NV

By this time, Afolabi was no longer able to surprise me. As surely as the sun came up, I could expect another e-mail proving that the crack they smoke in Nigeria puts ours in the shade.

Dear Stephanie,

Good day to you and how is your weekend? I am happy to hear your improvement but i need you to take things easy. I need you now to contact the bank. I have sent the details to you but you seem not to have done so. If you dont contact them then we cant proceed with these transfer and the money will be lost. I have told you in my last 4 mails to contact the bank but it seems you dont care about this business. See i am not hear to play games, we can play the games after we have collected the funds from the bank. If You dont call The bank by latest monday then we can forget about communication and this business. I hope you understand me. Do it immediately and mail me the latest

Olademeji O afolabi

I was getting tired of Afolabi, so I let him stew a while. Then I sent him this e-mail. Fans of James Thurber may enjoy the epizootic reference:

Dear Olademeji:

I hope you will pardon my long absence. I have been without cable service and the Internet for over a month!

It has been a total nightmare. Evidently my cable box was infested by a whole family of mongooses. They are a plague here in Nevada. I can't tell you how many times I have awakened and tried to put on my slippers and been bitten by mongooses curled up in the toes.

Anyway, my cousin Roy—I probably told you about his lawsuit over the faulty chin implant—came over and opened up on them with a can of pepper spray, and suddenly the air was filled with screaming mongooses. Roy was bitten multiple times, and as you are probably aware, mongooses carry the human variant of the disease that killed all the chestnut trees. And you can guess who had to pay for the shots.

It takes forever to get a cable box fixed out here, but I am back "online," and I must tell you, I just read some disturbing news. According to a newspaper in England, the cops in

Britain, or "Bobbies" as they are called, have just done a bunch of Nigerians much the same way as Roy did the mongooses. It says they arrested 500 of them for sending scam e-mails and getting foolish people to send them money.

Of course, I am terribly concerned for you. I am sure you are on the up and up as we say here in "the Colonies," but knowing how the police act in small silly countries, I would not be surprised if they had hauled you in by mistake.

Damn crazy foreigners. Present company excluded, of course.

Anyway, my dear, dear Olademeji, you must e-mail back and tell me what has become of you. And because I know how lonely men in prison can be (I correspond with a number of them), I have taken the liberty of attaching a "racy" picture of yours truly. I hope you enjoy it.

Your Stephie
Buttville, NV

Here is the (altered) photo I sent him:

And that, praise God, was the last I heard from him. But not the last he heard from me.

Stephie stood under a baobab tree on the sunny shore of Lake Zanzibar sipping her eighth or ninth sea breeze from the shell of a hollowed-out coconut. She watched the native fishermen as they waded in the shallows, stalking the enormous Tanganyikan bream that approached the beach to feed on spawning marabou conchs. As she struggled to focus, Jonny's polished chestnut shoulders emerged from the water. He strode toward her, adjusting his tiny, clingy magenta Speedo, the water falling away as he approached.

"I got someting for you, Stephie," Jonny said, winking slyly and reaching for a beach towel. He dried himself carefully, enjoying the sensation of her hungry eyes playing over his polished skin. He wrapped the towel around his waist and reached up under it with both hands. Suddenly the Speedo was on the sand, around his ankles. He stepped out of it, took her in his arms, and pressed her to him. "Now you gonna get it good, sister," he murmured in her burning ear.

He placed his hand on the small of her back, gave her a sly smile, shook his damp dreadlocks back out of his face, and moved his lips close to hers. She closed her eyes, waiting to be taken. Then she felt his hands relax and his body fall away. She opened her eyes and saw him lying crumpled on the ground before her. He was already snoring.

Unbelievable. ANOTHER worthless narcoleptic.

As soon as Robertson Savimbi disappeared, Jonny Etuwe grabbed his seat at the Internet café in Lagos and sent a message to Stephie.

From: "JONNY ETUWE"
Reply-To: jonnyetoobad@maytalls.net
Date: Sun Feb 2 18:18:47 2003
Subject: Fair Deal

FROM THE DESK OF Dr. JONNY ETUWE.

DEAR SIR,
WE ARE SENDING THIS LETTER **[SNIP, SNIP, SNIP]** ($41.5M
USD) . . .

THE OWNER OF THE ACCOUNT WILL BE COMPENSATED
WITH US$8.3 MILLION . . .

IT MAY INTEREST YOU TO KNOW THAT TWO YEARS AGO A
SIMILAR TRANSACTION WAS CARRIED OUT WITH ONE MR.
PATRICE MILLER

GOD BE WITH YOU AS I LOOK
FORWARD TO YOUR REPLY.

BEST REGARDS.
Dr, JONNY

Like all elderly women with nothing to do, Stephie is keen
on comparison shopping. So she sent Etuwe the following
message:

Dear Dr. Johnny:

Goodness, that's a lot of money! I would love to help you, but
I'm not sure I can! My savings account already has $410,000
in it, and I don't know if they'd let me put in another eight
million! I can ask on Monday. They don't mind answering
questions. Sometimes I call them just because I'm lonely.

May I ask what area of medicine you specialize in? I have had terrible problems with something called a "prolapse." I don't know if you know what that is, but it makes sitting a real problem, and I had to give up senior step aerobics after a humiliating incident. Western medicine has not helped at all, and I have been interested in tribal healing rituals ever since my childhood, when I saw them demonstrated in "Tarzan" movies.

Yours truly,

Mrs. Stephanie Hopkins
Coral Springs, Florida

Tarzan movies. Shame on me, I know. I couldn't help myself. There is just something unbelievably funny about a grown woman who thinks Johnny Weissmuller can talk to elephants.

Dr. Jonny responded with an exact duplicate of his previous e-mail. These Nigerians are so sharp, it amazes me their country isn't a superpower instead of being more like the world's spittoon.

I wrote back anyway.

Dear Dr. Jonny:

How wonderful to hear from you again! My prolapse is inflamed today, so I'm taking it easy; I really hope you can suggest a remedy. Sometimes backward people have hidden wisdom.

I think you are having a problem with Microsoft Outlook; this e-mail looks just like the one you sent yesterday.

As long as I'm writing, I must tell you, there is a problem with our deal. I have received an e-mail from Mrs. Robertson Savimbi of Angola, and—you will not believe this—he has a SIMILAR proposal! I can't believe my luck! I've never been lucky in the past! I haven't won anything since I was a girl and got a 4-H prize for growing the biggest capon in Himmler County. I used to hold its little head between my knees and feed it molasses with a funnel. Let's keep that between you and me.

Sorry to ramble. Must be my blood sugar.

Mrs. Savimbi offered me over thirty million dollars!!!!! I hate to look a gift horse in the mouth, but you are only offering eight, for the exact same service. Don't you think you and your friends could come up just a little bit? I was thinking fifteen. You would still have a lot for yourselves for buying the loud jewelry you people like so much.

God bless you and keep you. Word to your mother.

Stephanie Hopkins
Coral Springs, Florida

Again, I wanted to see if these guys were desperate enough to deal with an extremely obtuse lady who had apparently been in a coma during the civil rights movement. And Jonny did not disappoint.

Dear Stephanie Hopkins,
thanks for your mail and the content is well noted, please since you believe that your savings account can not take the fund, you can open a new current one that can accomodate the fund, i await your action in this regards.

Etuwe.

Well, isn't THAT exasperating? Jonny apparently didn't feel like discussing competitive propositions. Stephie had a proposition of her own.

Dear Dr. Jonny:

That is an excellent idea, and I will get right on it tomorrow.

Right now, I'm relaxing in a hot bath and wondering when we will meet to discuss our plans. I sent Consuelo home early, so I have the house to myself.

I don't know why, but I picture you as a handsome young man with broad shoulders, piercing brown eyes, and smooth ebony skin. I have always been fascinated by black men.

My Lawrence was a fine man and a good provider, but our romantic life was unsatisfying because unfortunately he had both infantile genitalia and narcolepsy.

The water is so warm and I feel so free with my house dress thrown over a towel rod and my support hose lying on the kitchen floor. Would you think less of me if I admitted I did not have both hands in plain view?

Oh, Jonny. If you can do this to me now, before we've ever met, I tremble to think of what will happen when we are together at last.

Hope you will call me. It would go so much faster if I could hear your voice: 305-443-08xx [number of a cleaning joint in South Miami that ruined THREE of my custom-made dress shirts].

Your Stephie
Coral Springs, Florida

Jonny either got wise or was too frightened to continue, so he and Stephie went their separate ways. But it wasn't long before Stephie got another spam. It came from the extraordinarily prolific Nigerian Internet celebrity, Maryam Abacha. Mrs. Abacha is the Nigerian Stephen King. Her literary works are probably responsible for a good 10 percent of e-mail traffic worldwide. Note the innovative mixing of ordinary text with classical Nigerian uppercase. For some reason, she instructed Stephie to send her reply to an attorney, Ben Kaita.

From: HER EXCELLENCY. DR MRS MARYAM ABACHA:

PRIVATE AND CONFIDENTIAL

MY DEAR,

IN THE NAME OF ALLAH, THE MOST GRACIOUS THE MOST MERCIFUL

It is with heart full of hope that I write to seek your help in the context below, I am Mrs. Maryam Abacha the second wife of the former Nigerian Head of state late General Sani Abacha whose Sudden death occurred on 8th of June 1998 . . .

. . . However, the new Democratic Government has on assumption of the office set up a panel of inquiry to the financial activities of my late husband (former Head of State) with a decision to freeze all his assets respectively . . . **[SNIP]**

Please all contacts must be made through my Lawyer Barrister BENSON KAITA Chambers via e-mail: ben_kaita35@rediffmail.com

I look forward to your quick response.

May Allah Bless You!

Best wishes,

Mrs. Maryam Abacha.

Stephie is an avid reader, gravitating mostly to romantic novels with covers featuring shirtless pirates in tight pants. But no one ever said she was a theologian.

Dear Mrs. Abacha

I am not clear on your salutation. You identify yourself as a woman, but you write in the name of "Allan"? Is he a business associate of yours? Whoever he is, you seem to have a high opinion of him!

I had no idea my little company appeared in the World Business Directory. I suppose my late husband Lawrence signed us up. Lawrence made Hopkins Hemorrhoid Clamps the industry leader by introducing milled titanium jaws, but if you are familiar with the company, you already know that.

I am sorry to hear you are having problems with the Democrats. They are driving us crazy over here in America, too, whining about the war and handing out rubber devices to our children. The war protesters are the worst. I think we need to keep sticking it to dirty heathen terrorists as much as possible, don't you? That's what my rabbi says, and I could not agree more. Just keep leveling mosques at random until we kill enough heathens to prove we mean business. That's what Teddy Roosevelt would have done.

I am flabbergasted by your offer. Can you seriously be offering me 2.2 million dollars for such a simple favor? Of course, I am very tempted. My hands are shaking as I type this, although that could be my thyroid medication. In order to make that kind of money in my regular business, I would have to have a Hopkins clamp on every backside in North America. What would I have to do for you?

Stephanie Hopkins
Vista del Mierda, Wyoming

Hold your stupid e-mails and fatwahs, please. I do not advocate leveling mosques. It's called "humor." Look it up. Ben got back to Stephie before too long.

From: BEN KAITA M:
Attn: Stephanie Hopkins,

thanks for your urgent reply to my clients cry for help to you, so to say my name is Barrister Benson kaita, i am the personal attorney to the former late head of states General Sani Abacha, may his gentle soul rest in perfect peace.

meanwhile i am including my official house, 1 aminu sariki street off sagbama Kano state and my number once again is 234-803-7407558.

As soon as i hear from you i will give you all the information and documents for you to file for this beneficial claim.

i await your urgent reply as soon as possible, also include your telephone number in your next mail to me so as to enable me call you as well.

thanks,

Benson Kaita (Barrister ESQ)

Barrister AND Esquire! So Benny was not merely a lawyer, but also an attorney. In addition. As well. Stephanie were impressed. But still, she wanted to know about Allan Akhbar.

Date: Tue, 25 May 2004 07:57:04 -0700 (PDT)
From: "Steve H."
Subject: Re: sorry for the delay in contacting you.
To: "BEN KAITA M"

Dear Benny:

I am glad you are not writing to me in the name of Allan again. I found that very confusing. If Allan wants to correspond with me, he can write me himself. I am an old lady subject to spells, and I do not need the aggravation of sifting through intermediaries.

I am very excited by your e-mail. I could use some spare capital right now. I refuse to touch the $950,000 my late husband Lawrence left me, but I have a great project I would like to get going. My friend Mabel and I thought it would be great fun to sell chia pets in erotic shapes. Isn't that hilarious? I wonder why no one ever thought of it before. Talk about a conversation piece.

I got a toll-free number put in so my grandkids can call me from college and so on. Please feel free to use it. My number is 800-997-xxxx [Customer Service, Preparation H]. If I do not answer, I am probably not here or knocked out on Halcyon. But my housekeeper Consuelo will pick up. Her English is okay if you speak slowly. She sounds a bit masculine because she represented El Salvador in the hammer throw in the 1975 Olympics, and the steroids deepened her voice and exacerbated her facial hair problem.

But she is good as gold and will gladly take down your information.

Stephanie Hopkins
Vista del Mierda, Wyoming

While I was waiting for Benny and Allan Akhbar to respond, I cranked off a couple more e-mails under other identities. I got a letter from Chief Okunday Something-or-Other, and being a huge fan of *Dr. Strangelove*, I decided to reply as one of my favorite movie characters.

By the way, the Chief turned out to be a pal of one of General Abacha's cronies. Small world. Here's part of his e-mail.

For the purpose of introduction, I am the private attorney to GENERAL ISHAYA BAMAYI, the former chief of army staff during the regime of late general Sani Abacha, who was the former head of state.

As you may know, General Bamayi is presently in detention over some activities that took place when he was in government and the matter in court right now.

It was only fitting that another general answer an e-mail like that.

Dear Chief:

I thank you for this offer. As a former military man, I have no doubt that your story is true. I am familiar with the way things work in backward little countries such as yours, and I am not surprised at all that General Bamayi would abscond with funds belonging to his yammering, barefoot compatriots. And I have no moral objections. He can invest wisely and provide for his family's security, whereas they would just blow it all on boomboxes and colorful trinkets.

I will be happy to assist you in any way possible, provided it is not necessary for me to come into contact with any beverages other than grain alcohol and rainwater. I am sure you understand without further explanation.

As it happens, I have a toll-free number for my operatives to use in connection with our efforts to fight the insidious fluoridation of water. That number is 888-303-xxxx [Sharpton 2004 Headquarters]. I must insist that you guard that number with your life; its security is vital to the purity of America's water supply and that of our very bodies. Contact me immediately so we can begin our mission.

God willing, we will prevail in peace and freedom from fear and in true health through the purity and essence of our precious bodily fluids.

Yours sincerely,

General Jack Ripper, USAF (Ret.)

Okunday vanished, but Ben and Allan Akhbar returned:

From: BEN KAITA M:
attn: steve H.

Madam,

i write to know if you are still interested in this deal, please tell me so that i can proceed with the document.

regards

Benson.

Interested? Hell, yes, she was interested. Stephie never saw an e-mail scam that didn't get her little wheels turning.

I thought an interesting disease might excuse her neglect.

Benny:

I am so sorry I did not get back to you sooner. I hope you and Mr. Allan Akhbar are well.

I have been unable to answer my e-mail for over a month. I went to my brother's ranch for a weekend and helped him inseminate some mares, and unbelievably, I contracted equine syphilis, which gave me a nasty rash on both hands. I would have dictated an e-mail to Consuelo, but she is an ignorant foreigner and cannot type. I wish everyone could be a well-educated and hygienic American like myself, but I guess I will just have to get used to the fact that foreigners are backward and don't always smell so good.

Anyway, the penicillin ointment has worked its magic, and I am ready to help in any way I can.

Stephanie Hopkins
Vista del Mierda, Wyoming

Maybe it was the tardiness. Maybe it was the syphilis. But something put Ben and Allan off, and that was the end of that.

"Mr. Perkins?" Toynbee inquired, his nose just inside the barely cracked door, "Do you have a moment? The letter from Mr. Hopkins has arrived." "By all means, Toynbee," said Perkins, "bring it here so I can have a look at it." "I've reviewed the letter," said Toynbee, "and I think I should warn you that some of the language is perplexing." He handed Perkins the letter gingerly, still standing a good distance away. "Heavens, man," said Perkins, "come closer. I'm not a bomb."

Perkins perused the letter. "Ah," he said, "I believe I see what you're referring to. He has interrupted the second paragraph by gratuitously inserting the words 'nipples,' 'buttocks,' and 'mangina.' " "Yes, sir," said Toynbee, "those were the terms which concerned me." "Not to worry, Toynbee," said Perkins, "Shipman said this sort of thing was to be expected."

Okay, don't make fun of me, because I am going to reveal something very personal and very painful. I have a disability.

No, I am not referring to my looks.

Perhaps you have heard of Tourette's syndrome. Sufferers blurt out all sorts of obscene exclamations at random intervals. There have been times when I have almost envied them. Especially in my work as an attorney.

JUDGE: "Mr. Graham, your argument is airtight and impeccably researched, and you did a magnificent job of presenting it. However, I am going to rule against you because judges can do whatever they want, and I am retaining water. Do you have any questions?"

ME: "No, your honor FAT HO FAT FAT SEA COW CROW'S FEET LARDASS, I think I understand."

Anyway, it turns out there is a second variant of Tourette's. Read about it yourself.

Dear Friend,

My name is Mr. Ian Shipman (A British Citizen), I work in a bank here in the Germany with a corresponding office in UK.

I am contacting you on business transfer of a huge sum of money from a deceased account, though I know that a transaction of this magnitude will make anyone apprehensive and worried, but I am assuring you that all will be well at the conclusion of this transaction I decided to contact you due to the urgency of this transaction . . .

I am the account officer of a foreigner named Mr & Mrs. Raymond Beck in our UK branch office before I move to Germany for official assignment. Mr. Raymond Beck died long with his wife in the plane crash of 31 October, 1999 on board the Egyptian Airline 9 90 alongside other passengers.

Please consult the Cable News Network (CNN) website below for verification.

http://www.cnn.com/US/9911/02/egyptair990.list/index.html or http://216.157.75.11/discus/messages/1073/400.html? 1086886167

Since his death, none of his next-of-kin or relations has come forward to lay claims to this money as the heir . . .

Please reply to shipman2005@zwallet.com

Best regards,
Ian Shipman.

At the time I received this e-mail, none of my imaginary characters had any handicaps. This was before Steve Hopkins lost his prostate gland and Stephie grew her congenital twin. I resolved to correct the shameful imbalance. In the name of diversity.

Dear Mrs. Shipman:

Your offer is unbelievable and I am HIGHLY interested, but frankly, I doubt you will wish to do business with me. I have a freakish disability which is likely to put you off. Although some cruel people claim I am making it up.

Perhaps you have heard of Tourette's syndrome, the disability which causes people to blurt out strange things without realizing it. Well, there is a variant of the disease that applies to typing. Sometimes I type offensive things for no reason, without realizing it, and I do not notice them when I proofread, because that is part of the syndrome.

It is very sad, because I have medical bills I need to pay and I cannot hold a regular job.

But if you are willing to overlook my problem, I would be very, very eager to help and most cooperative!

Thanks for the offer. Truthfully, I do not expect to hear ASS LIMEY [CENSORED] TEATS back from you.

Steve Hopkins
Monadnock Falls, WY

And to prove just how stupid and determined e-mail scammers are, I now present the astonishing response.

From: "shipman andrees"
Subject: Re: am okay
Date: Tue, 27 Jul 2004 13:39:51 +0000

Hello steve,
please can you fish me with your datas, that is pnone no fax and others.
Rrgard,
Shipman

I decided Shipman needed another blast.

Dear Mrs. Shipman:

I cannot tell you how touched I am that you wrote back. I am so used to people reading my e-mails and getting furious at me or ridiculing me for this sad condition, which I cannot help; I am full of emotion to see that you are willing to treat me with dignity. I am embarrassed to say I cried a little. I am so lonely, and you are being so nice to me.

In your e-mail you mention a fax, but I did not see anything about a fax number. Can you please tell me where to send the RECTAL! RECTAL! [CENSORED]! materials?

Steve Hopkins
Monadnock Falls, WY

I'm still waiting for him to send me that fax number.

Let me start my next disability-related segment by asking you a rhetorical question. You know what's really low? I mean, lower than a whale booger on the bottom of the Pacific Ocean? Getting at people by picking on their children.

Of course, that doesn't mean I have a problem with it.

Witness my exchange with Edward Smith. I don't have all of it. I let a Yahoo! account go inactive, and I lost some of the e-mails and all of the headers, but you will just have to believe me. This is a real guy.

Dear friend,

I am Mr Edward Smith the personal driver to Mr Robert Brown the director of Highbrons construction company contracted under the ministry of mines and power for the completion of the last phase of the multi billion dollars Ajaokuta steel project here in Nigeria.

I have been his chauffer for the past twelve years and before his departure six months ago to Italy for the procurement of some of the industrial machineries for the Ajaokuta project completion we the workers has not been paid which made the workers union to go on strike . . .

After buying the fruits and was coming back to the car he looked right and left there was no car though there was a bend and immediately he entered the road to cross over a car came out from that very bend and that was the end of my master because he was rushed to the hospital though it was too late to save his life . . .

As the driver i had not option than to force open the briefcase which is still inside the car and discovered a huge amount of money infact at first i got confused . . .

I will stop here until, I receive your response.

Thanks and God bless.
Mr Edward Smith.

I guess the name "Robert Brown" is just plain unlucky. If your name is Robert Brown, either you get run over by a drunk Nigerian out on a joy ride, or you end up married to Whitney Houston and you can't walk across your kitchen without stepping on a crack pipe. As it happened, I could relate to Mr. Smith's terrible loss.

Dear Mr. Smith:

My heart goes out to you concerning the untimely death of Mr. Brown. I am especially touched, as I, too, have lost a good friend to a violent accident. My mah jongg partner Mabel was marching in a gay pride parade two years ago when she lost her footing and was crushed by the "Celebrating Tom Cruise" float. The worst part is that her screams were drowned out by the float's speakers, which were blasting "In the Navy" at high volume. So she was dragged for several blocks.

We have dangerous roadside fruit stands here in America, too, and it always amazes me that people will risk their lives, dodging cars to get an ear of corn and a bag of rancid turnips.

It is thoughtful and responsible of you to continue going to work, what with no one to drive for. Not many people would be that dedicated.

How exactly can I help you? I can't afford a chauffeur, although I can always use someone to tidy up the yard and hose out the mongoose pens.

Stephanie Hopkins
Chickenlips, IA

After writing a certain number of Nigerians, a guy can't help but get a little cocky. There had been a time when I would have been too timid to claim I lived in a town called "Chickenlips," but by the time Ed arrived, I had really hit my spammer-tormenting stride. I felt invincible.

And what is it about mongooses? I cannot resist their pull.

I no longer have the e-mail in which I asked Ed for a photo, but thank goodness, I saved the photo itself. Ed was a proud family man, and he sent this shot of himself with his wife and daughters.

I wasn't sure how to respond. I considered saying something like, "My, how many wives you have! How do you keep them all satisfied?" But that was too easy. I decided to call in one of my spammer aliases, Chuku Peter (more about him later). And I made up a new imaginary girlfriend, Mrs. Busch. First name: Rose.

Dear Ed:

We have a serious problem.

I received your photo, and I was very excited. I was at the beauty salon talking about it with my friend Rose, and I showed her a printout of the photo. She was extremely disturbed. Apparently, she received an offer similar to yours from a Nigerian named Chuck Peters (chukupeterbutthead@yahoo.com), and he sent her the EXACT

SAME PHOTO. She forwarded it from WebTV, and I am attaching it so you can see.

He also included a message, which I will copy here.

>DEAR MRS. BUSCH:

>THANK YOU DEAR FOR THE EMAIL. I HOPE BY THE GRACE OF
>GOD THAT THE FLUID HAS DRAINED AND YOU ARE ONCE AGAIN
>ABLE TO FASTEN YOUR SHOES.
>
>AS YOU REQUESTED I HAVE SENT A PHOTO OF ME AND MY
>FAMILY. ALTHOUGH YOUNG EFFIWAT (THE CHILD IN THE
>MIDDLE) IS QUITE ILL, WERE ABLE TO GET HER OUT OF BED
>AND INCLUDE HER. YOU CAN CLEARLY SEE THAT THE CHILD
>IS NOT RIGHT. NOTE THE LISTLESS STARE. FORTUNATELY,
>HER FROCK CONCEALS THE EXTRA LEG.
>
>THE CATHOLIC CHARITY DOCTOR ASSURES US HE CAN REMOVE
>THE LEG AND THAT THE BRAIN TUMOR CAN BE EXCISED WITH
>NO ILL EFFECTS, HOWEVER HE CANNOT BEGIN UNTIL HE
>RECEIVES $1200 USD FOR THE NEW GENERATOR. ONCE THIS
>IS DONE WE CAN GO ON AND EMPLOY VARIOUS MODALITIES TO
>GET YOUR FUNDS RELEASED TO YOU.

Rose and I are quite confused. If you would like to prove you are telling the truth, please send the photo I asked for previously, with you holding a sign with the name of the Masters & Johnson law firm on it. That would remove all doubt. Otherwise, I cannot go forward.

I am sorry there are such dishonest people in the world, but I know of no other solution.

God Bless.

Stephie Hopkins

Ed was incensed that another Nigerian would stoop to stealing his family. And saying those things about his daughter! That was an outrage. There was nothing wrong with the girl, apart from looking like Steve Urkel in drag.

BE CAREFUL OF E-MAIL HACKERS BECAUSE THEY WILL RUIN YOU.

Dear Stephanie,

How are you today? I want you to be cautious of email hackers okay.

The chukupeterbutthead@yahoo.com is a fake because how can a banker operate @ yahoo.com account instead of a bank account?

What really happened is a coincidence because after i sent you my picture since i told you that i was new to computer usage i was ignorant of removing my picture from the computer programmes and someone else entered into the computer profile and took my picture and sent to your friend okay.

You know that i have no personal computer in my house.

To be on the safer side just tell your friend never to communicate with chukupeter or whatever he calls himself again for security reasons . . .

Cant you see for yourself that the idiot has in disguise started asking you for us$1200 for the treatment of his mother not my daughter?

I still maintain my stand that i may not be able to hold a picture with a placard in my hand just because of this flimsy reason . . .

I am not after your money like the stupid email hacker but just to use your position to get the money into America since human right is observed over there and there is stability in government unlike here in Africa.

Please reply this message very urgent as i am very worried.

Thanks and God bless.

Mr Edward Smith.

I honestly think that these guys would believe me if I said Stephie had wings and performed in air shows.

The best way to drive a Nigerian spammer out of his mind is to convince him that you're giving money to another Nigerian spammer. Look what I told poor Ed.

Oh, Edward.

I am so embarrassed. I sent Mr. Peters the $1200.

You must think I'm a terrible fool! I suppose I am.

My heart just went out to that girl. I mean, what if what he is saying about her is true? She is just now reaching the age where she should be trying out for the cheerleading squad and developing an interest in boys and going to dances, and here she is with brain tumors and a third leg! Even if a boy asks her out, that will all be over the minute he sees her in a bathing suit.

Oh, I know he's probably a liar. But I could not take that chance. But my late husband Morris left me his drive-in medical waste business, so $1200 is not much money to me, and if it could help some poor deformed girl get her first date, then it is well worth it.

When I was a young girl, I was severely disfigured by chronic inguinal granulomas, so I know the pain this girl is going through, if she actually exists. My condition cleared up on its own, but that is not likely to happen to a third leg.

I am having a very hard time deciding what to do now. I will get back to you when I make up my mind. The picture I asked for would certainly help, but I understand if you can't do it.

Stephie Hopkins
Chickenlips, IA

That message got Ed pretty riled up. But while he questioned my judgment, he admired my generous spirit. Is there such a thing as an "inguinal granuloma"?

THE GIRL IN THE PICTURE IS MY DAUGHTER AND NOTHING IS WRONG WITH HER PLEASE FOR CHRIST SAKE.

As i just got into the cyber cafe to check if you had responded i received your mail.

It is good to help those that have problem but please be it known to you that none of my daughters had such a problem okay.

I have told you several times to give to me your phone number so that i will call you and you do not want to give me your phone number are you hiding yourself?

Please tell me if you do not want to be part of this so that i will look for someone else than waiting in vain for you.

Thanks and God bless you for your urgent response to this message.

Best regards,

Edward Smith.

I love it when they threaten to do business with someone else. Like I'm going to be jealous when the moron down the street sends them ten thousand dollars and ends up a ward of the state.

Dear Edward:

I know you claim the girl in the photo is your daughter, but look at the e-mail I just got from Chuck Peters.

> DEAR DEAR STEPHANIE:

> MY HEART OVERFLOWS WITH GRATITUDE AND I WISH
> TO THANK YOU BY EVERY POSSIBLE MODALITY.
> THE OPERATION WAS A SUCCESS AND NOW THERE
> IS HOPE THAT YOUNG EFFIWAT WILL SOMEDAY
> ATTRACT A MAN AND HAVE CHILDREN INSTEAD OF
> BEING A CURIOSITY EXHIBITED IN CARNIVALS AND SUCH.

> YOUR OBSERVATIONS ARE CORRECT. HER HEAD IS QUITE
> LARGE, HER TEMPLES BULGE, AND THE LEFT EYE WANDERS
> HORRIBLY. BUT THE DOCTOR SAYS THAT WILL CHANGE
> NOW THAT THE TUMORS ARE GONE AND THE FLUID IS
> REMOVED.

> SHE WILL HAVE TO REMAIN IN THE CHARITY HOSPITAL
> FOR 6 MOS. WHILE SHE RECOVERS. UNFORTUNATELY
> SHE WILL HAVE LITTLE TO DO, AS A LORRY RAN
> OVER HER SAXOPHONE. THERE IS A NICE ONE AVAILABLE
> NEARBY FOR 750 USD, BUT WHY AM I TELLING YOU THIS,
> AS IT IS NOT YOUR CONCERN.

> GOD BLESS

> CHUKU PETER
> chukupeterbutthead@yahoo.com

I suppose it is possible that he is lying, but I feel good because I did the right thing. I also sent the money for the saxophone; I hope she enjoys it.

I am still considering your proposition.

Stephie

I really wish I hadn't lost all those e-mails, like a dumbass, because Ed sent me ten more messages after that. "I WILL GIVE YOU ONE MORE CHANCE." "VERY WORRIED. PLEASE WRITE." He was a rude little bastard, so I quit fooling with him. Long story short, he never got a dime.

And so far, little Effie's third leg has not grown back.

Steve held his can of Olde English 800 safely above his head and stepped warily past the angry emu. It had allowed little Skeezicks to tickle its narrow, bony forehead, bending down and making happy trilling noises, but something about Steve rubbed it the wrong way. It gobbled menacingly at him and pawed the dust like a fighting bull.

Steve turned and stood his ground. He hadn't beaten strokes, cancer, and type 2 diabetes just to have his ass kicked by a big hairy duck.

Have you ever been to a petting zoo? My dad can't stand them. When we were kids, he was one of those dads who only stops the car when a wheel falls off or someone important (i.e., him) has to pee, and we only got him to stop at tourist attractions two or three times on the dozens of trips we made between Florida and Kentucky.

Once we managed to get him to pull over at one of the many roadside zoos that used to line the highways going up the middle of the state. Mom, my sister, and I went in to see the animals ("a one-eyed monkey and a dog with an infected ear," said Dad), and we left Dad in the parking lot with my sister's aging poodle, Boof.

Boof was eight years old when a friend of my sister's palmed him off on us. He was blind in one eye, and he had some kind of tumor that had enlarged his right testicle to the size of a tennis ball. But he refused to die, and he bit everyone he could catch. Dad hated Boof, and the feeling was mutual.

Boof was irate that he had been left to rot in the heat with Dad, and he strained on his leash, making ear-splitting poodle screeches at the animals inside the zoo. For a time, Dad sat out there and endured it, but patience was never his long suit. He soon decided he had had enough. He unhooked Boof from the leash and let the little son of a bitch go. At least that's what my mother claims. He denies it.

Boof skittered into the zoo as fast as his arthritic pins would carry him, and he went through the place barking at a pitch that could shatter glass and trying to get through the chicken wire to eat the horrified monkeys. Some of the animals got mad, and the rest were scared, and every creature in the place, including the sideshow-grade fat lady who worked the door, started running in circles and breaking things and screaming bloody murder.

Dad was hoping Boof would get too close to a chimp and get his little head twisted off, but my idiot sister retrieved him, and the fat lady made us leave, and I don't think my mother spoke to Dad until we got to South Carolina.

Me, I thought it was a damn good try.

You will see the relevance shortly.

Date: Mon, 29 Aug 2005 06:11:29 -0700 (PDT)
From: "w williamson" >annfatlady@gob.com>
To: annfatlady@gob.com
Subject: Kindly Reply

From: Mrs Ann williamson
#23 Les Caches
St. Martins
Guernsey.
Channel Islands,
United Kingdom.

I am the above named person but now undergoing medical treatment in London, England. I am married to Dr. Richard K. Williamson who worked with British Railway Commission in Chelsea England for over a decade before he died on 5th of July in the year 2003. We were married for fifteen years without a child. He died after a brief illness that lasted for two weeks. Before his death he made a vow to use his wealth for the down trodden and the less privileged in the society.

Since his death I decided not to re-marry or get a child outside my matrimonial home. When my late husband was alive he deposited the sum of £7.5 Million (Seven Million and Five Hundred Thousand pounds) with one Finance House and Presently, this money is still with the Finance House. Recently, I found out that I had cancer, which my doctors said that I am still lucky to be leaving. Though what disturbs me most is my stroke.

Having known my condition I decided to donate this fund to an individual or better still a God fearing person who will utilize this money the way I am going to instruct herein. I want an individual that will use this to fund and provide succor to poor and indigent persons, orphanages, and widows and for propagating peace in the universe.

I understand that blessed is the hand that giveth. I took this decision because I do not have any child that will inherit this money and my husband relatives are not inclined to helping poor persons and I do not want my husbands hard earned money to be misused or spent in the manner in which my late husband did not specify. I do not want a situation where this money will be used in an ungodly manner, hence the reason for taking this bold decision. I am not afraid of death hence I know where I am going. I know that I am going to be in the bossom of the Almighty. I do not need any telephone communication in this regard because of my health, and because of the presence of my husband's relatives around me always. I do not want them to know about this development. With God all things are possible.

As soon as I receive your reply I shall give you the contact of the Finance House. I will also issue you a letter of authority that will empower you as the original beneficiary of this fund. I want you to always pray for me. My happiness is that I lived alife worthy of emulation.

Whosoever that wants to serve the Almighty must serve him with all his heart and mind and always be prayerful all through your life. Any delay in your reply will give me room in sourcing for an individual for this same purpose. Please assure me that you will act according to specification herein.

Hoping to hear from you.

Thank you and May the Almighty bless you.

Anna williamson.
{Direct email annfatlady@fatscape.com}

It always amazes me how these terminally ill Nigerians somehow find the energy to write 5,000 words of tear-jerking copy. My heart went out to Mrs. Williamson, and although I am not a doctor, I offered the best health advice I could.

Dear Mrs. Williamson:

It saddens my heart to hear about your medical problems. It seems like you just can't catch a break.

Before I go on to the part about the money, let me ask if you have ever heard of a product called the Juiceman. This thing is simply incredible. It was invented by a scrawny, bandy-legged old geezer who had a long list of diseases such as cancer, cataracts, an enlarged prostate, bad knees, psoriasis, plantar warts, and severe, crippling constipation. He somehow managed to drag himself to his workbench and make an amazing machine that will extract the juice from practically anything. He juiced fruits, vegetables, and God knows what else, and after a few months of drinking this stuff, he was completely cured.

He does promotional shows for the machine, and he comes out and does exercises and dances and so on. I mean, it's not like Gene Kelly or anything—he sort of shuffles around in a circle—but it's pretty impressive for a guy who, a few years ago, could have been killed by someone yelling "BOO."

The machine is unbelievable. Ordinary juicers just juice oranges and such, but this thing will juice anything that contains water. Until this machine came along, things like potato juice and turnip juice were impossible to come by. Although having had them, I cannot say there was a great need to obtain them.

Doctors won't tell you about juicing, because all they care about is taking your money. They actually want you to get worse and then die. But I've been using my juice machine for several years now, and I feel stronger and healthier than ever. Although during that time, I did have a couple of strokes and a bout with cancer, which resulted in the loss of a section of my colon. And last month I was diagnosed with diabetes.

Anyway, it worked for me, and I thought you might want to hear about it.

I am very interested in your proposal because it would enable me to go out and do some good in my community. For a long time now, I have wanted to go out on the street and minister to the local prostitutes. We already have a good rapport, and I think I could be very effective if I had something to offer them other than talk and IOUs.

Please let me know how to proceed. These ladies have no one else to turn to, and they can use the extra income now that the rendering plant has been closed.

Steve Hopkins
Hominy Falls, PA

Did you know that constipation really *can* be crippling? It's not a subject I want to dwell on, but apparently some folks go so long without taking a deuce, they have to be opened up. The doctors go in there with a trenching tool or something. When I think about that, the huge serving of oatmeal I eat every morning suddenly seems easier to face.

Anna was real grateful to hear from me, yada yada yada.

Date: Fri, 09 Sep 2005 08:10:44 -0400
From: annfatlady@fatscape.com
To: "Steve H." <xxxxxxxx@yahoo.com>
Subject: Thank you for your thoughtfulness

Dear Steve,

Let me start with saying thanks for the time you took to go through my mail and also for the thoughtfulness to assist in this case I am really grateful may the peace of our good Lord be with you. Due to the my failing health its difficult for me to always check my mails promptly because I am always in bed, due to the hash medications I am subjected to, so pardon me for the delay in replying you.

However like I did explain to you in my first mail, my late husband Dr. Richard Key deposited the sum of USD 9.1 million, which I had to convert the equivalent to GBP 7.5

million. This fund is deposited in The Netherlands in a finance house, which the funds where deposited in a private safe. After his death I discovered that his family became greedy they wanted me to release all documents regarding all his transactions which I declined because I know they want to take everything for themselves.

This has been a very difficult situation not knowing whom to trust. I decided to look for someone outside to use these funds for the less privileged.

[SNIP]

Once again permit me to thank you for the heart and willingness to assist in this case. I am really grateful. I will be expecting to hear from you soon.

Cheers,

Anna

Did you catch that? Anna said she was in bed all the time because of her "hash medications." I can see her now, lying on her back in a room plastered with blacklight posters, listening to Seals & Crofts.

I was pretty excited to learn that Anna planned to subsidize my philanthropic outreach to the local prostitutes. I sent her the Al Franken passport.

Date: Tue, 13 Sep 2005 10:28:26 -0700 (PDT)
From: "Steve H." <xxxxxxxx@yahoo.com>
Subject: Re: Thank you for your thoughtfulness
To: annfatlady@fatscape.com

Dear Anna:

I am very glad to be of assistance. I hope you looked into that juicing thing. The old guy who sells the machines still looks fit as a fiddle, although his eyebrows appear to be growing at an abnormal rate.

I am attaching a copy of my international passport!

I am very excited about ministering to the local girls who work down by the docks. Last night I took it upon myself to cash in a savings bond and invite six of them to a local motel so I could minister to them in privacy—really minister their brains out—complete with anointing oil (flavored) and laying on of hands. We laid hands on each other pretty vigorously until the unbelievers downstairs complained about the music and thumping sounds and we were forced to end the revival prematurely.

I really think that with your help, I can do these unfortunate ladies a world of good. And they, me.

Steve Hopkins
Hominy Falls, PA

As older chicks go, Anna was pretty broad minded. She had no problems with my work, which gave new meaning to the term "lay ministry." She sent me a photo of herself and her late husband. I felt sure I had seen him before. Have you ever seen the Eddie Murphy movie, *Trading Places*?

Date: Thu, 15 Sep 2005 08:59:48 -0400
From: annfatlady@fatscape.com
To: "Steve H." <xxxxxxxx@yahoo.com>
Subject: I received the copy of passport

Dear Steve Hopkins,

How are you and you family? Thanks for finally replying to my mail. I received a copy of your passport, you are such a handsome man. I selected you because I know you leave outside the United Kingdom this makes it better for me to use you for this cause. I am doing this because I do not want my greedy in-laws whose intentions are to grab everything my late husband worked for. They never cared about us, they never wanted their brother to be married to me, why, they fund out I was not able to bear children because of my health but yet still he loved me all the way, he was strong for me and I stood by him. They want me to release all documents regarding his transactions, which I have declined to knowing perfectly well who these people are, they will just squander this wealth for their selfish purpose. I know they are waiting for me to die, I know that. A None is praying for me all the want is money. If I leave these funds with them I know that they will not use it as I specify, this is the reason I have contacted you.

So please I want you to be strong for me, because I dont want these people to know what I am up to and also do not want to leave this funds for them either. I really appreciate the good work you are doing in concealing and ministering to these young people, it really makes me know you are a very positive person, and enjoys doing something good for humanity, I do appreciate the work keep it up.

I have also forwarded your details to my lawyer to prepare a Memorandum of Understanding {MOU} and Letter of Administration in your favour as the beneficiary, which he will be, forwarding to you soon. you can also contact him to introduce yourself to him, his name is Edward Dickson {Hill Dickson-Attorney at law}, Phone number: +44 7768 216 689.

I have also attached a copy of my picture and that of my late husband for your viewing, with the death certificate and also the certificate of deposit. Kindly confirm if you got them.

Bye for now,

Cheers

Anna

That is one cool photo. I wonder who those people really are.

"Still he loved me all the way," she said. I'll just bet he did.

I was tired of Anna, so I quit writing her, but she kept pestering me, probably because I was the only person who had ever been stupid enough to answer her. I decided to get back in touch, and I had an excellent reason for the delay.

Date: Thu, 29 Sep 2005 15:08:47 -0700 (PDT)
From: "Steve H." <xxxxxxxx@yahoo.com>
Subject: Re: I received the copy of passport
To: annfatlady@fatscape.com

Dear Anna:

Please forgive me for delaying. The most incredible thing happened. I took my nephew Skeezicks to the local petting zoo, and while he was stroking a prairie dog, an emu bit me through the bars of its enclosure. I don't know if you are familiar with these creatures; they are enormous flesh-eating birds from Tasmania.

Anyway, it broke the skin, and the local health authorities insisted on quarantining me because these birds are known to carry fulminating erysipelas, also known as Yanni's disease. I told them they ought to quarantine the sons of bitches who ran the zoo, but they got a stick and forced me into the van.

Thank you for the photo. Your late husband resembles the famous American actor Ralph Bellamy. Perhaps you have seen him in movies such as "Donkey Punch Summer" or "Dr. Pemberton and His Musical Pants."

Your lawyer friend has not contacted me yet.

Steve Hopkins
Hominy Falls, PA

He had probably contacted me fifty times. I always say they haven't contacted me. Drives them nuts. Here is an e-mail I actually responded to.

From: "Hill Dickson" <hilldickson@fatladyaccomplice.com>
To: xxxxxxxx@yahoo.com
CC: annfatlady@fatscape.com
Date: Mon, 03 Oct 2005 06:24:49 -0500
Subject: From Edward Dickson

Attn: Stephen Hopkins,

My client Mrs. Anna Williamson requested that I forward to you this LETTER OF ADMINISTRATION and MEMORANDUM OF UNDERSTANDING for your viewing and also I would want you to study and inform me if acceptable. Kindly find in your attachment the copies of the documents.

Thanks,

Edward Dickson Esq.
Hill Dickson Attorney at Law
Pearl Assurance House Derby Square, Liverpool
Phone: + 44 77 68 216 689
Fax: + 44 87 1247 4343

I took my sweet time getting back to him. I figured the emu story would work twice. Did you know they have a drug now that cures Yanni's disease? Word up. I told Ed about it.

Date: Mon, 10 Oct 2005 11:54:59 -0700 (PDT)
From: "Steve H." <xxxxxxxx@yahoo.com>
Subject: Re: From Edward Dickson
To: "Hill Dickson" <hilldickson@fatladyaccomplice.com>

Dear Ed:

Sorry not to get back to you sooner. I have had another difficult week. After being quarantined for fulminating erysipelas after that devastating emu bite, I thought I had a clean bill of health, but then the telltale pustules appeared around my nipples, and they chased me into the van again and made me take a course of antibiotics. Regrettably, the only effective antibiotic, craptomycetin, is only available in the US in livestock feed, so I was forced to eat emu chow several times per day. The resulting gas is beyond description, but you probably don't want to hear about that.

I am sorry to tell you the Memo of Understanding came through as a corrupted file [what a lie]. What is it exactly that I am supposed to understand? I hope there is no math involved.

Did Anna forward my passport photo? If not, let me know, and I will send it. If you wish, I can forward some other shots. I have a couple where I'm wearing sort of a catsuit . . . anyway, let me know.

Steve Hopkins
Hominy Falls, PA

One of these days, the Yanni's disease bug will develop a resistance to craptomycetin, and then EVERYONE'S nipples will be in jeopardy.
Ed felt my pain.

From: "Hill Dickson" <hilldickson@fatladyaccomplice.com>
To: "Steve H." <xxxxxxxx@yahoo.com>
Date: Tue, 11 Oct 2005 08:01:17 -0500
Subject: From Edward Dickson

Hello Mr. Stephen Hopkins,

I have waited for quite a long time for your response, sorry for your condition. My client Mrs. Anna Williamson is also very worried about you. I hope you feel better now after ondergoing those prescriptions.

In response to your mail I have attached another signed copy of the MOU and LETTER OF ADMINISTRATION, for you to go through and sign if acceptable by you {The MOU has detailed out the process of this transaction, while the Letter Of Admin, is empowering you to the estate}.

I will be awiating your immedite reply.

Kind Regards,

Edward Dickson Esq.

Craptomycetin is a wonder drug, but it takes a while to work. My symptoms were gradually disappearing. He sent me a couple of beautiful PDF documents to sign, but they aren't funny enough to republish.

Date: Fri, 14 Oct 2005 13:48:44 -0700 (PDT)
From: "Steve H." <xxxxxxxx@yahoo.com>
Subject: Re: From Edward Dickson
To: "Hill Dickson" <hilldickson@fatladyaccomplice.com>

Mr. Dickson:

I am in receipt of your documents.

Thank you for your concern. I am feeling much better now. The hot flashes appear to be abating, although I am still subject to odd dreams caused by a peculiar sensitivity to the antibiotics. Last night I dreamed I was a pair of gold lamé tap pants belonging to the American celebrity Wink Martindale.

Mr. Martindale is a remarkable man. Most Americans know him only as a game show host, but he also invented the solar-powered penile implant, which has been a blessing to retirees in Florida and Arizona.

I am not totally sure what to do with these documents. Perhaps you can inform me. One of them says I have to use the money for various charities. I don't see any mention of my favorite, which is my one-on-one ministry to inexpensive ladies of the evening, but I suppose that would be covered by the HIV thing. The way some of these girls live just breaks your heart. I was talking to a motel desk clerk about it last night and I think we both got a little misty eyed.

Mrs. Williamson seems like a very nice lady. Please tell her I am fine and that the carbuncles have stopped seeping.

Steve Hopkins

Wink Martindale is supposedly a great guy, but he has the biggest teeth you ever saw. When he used to smile at contestants, it actually scared me. I think he could bite your arm clean off. Him or Carly Simon.

You can tell these guys like a thousand times that you need instructions, and they always believe it.

From: "Hill Dickson" <hilldickson@fatladyaccomplice.com>
1:To: "Steve H." <xxxxxxxx@yahoo.com>
Date: Mon, 17 Oct 2005 03:01:02 -0500
Subject: From Edward Dickson

Attn: Mr. Stephen Hopkins,

In respect to your mail I believe that my client Mrs Anna Williamson has explained what you need to do with the funds when it gets to you just as the MOU has indicated. All you need to do is to endorse the documents and send back to me to enable me forward to you the contacts of the security firm so that you can resume comunication with them.

I will need you to also call me of send me your phone number to enable us communicate.

Thanks,

Edward Dickson Esq.

I was all out of emu stories, so I let the whole thing drop.
But months later, I decided to torment them just a little
more. Naturally, I blamed them for the hiatus.

Date: Tue, 31 Jan 2006 09:18:24 -0800 (PST)
From: "Steve H." <xxxxxxxx@yahoo.com>
Subject: Re: From Edward Dickson
To: "Hill Dickson" <hilldickson@fatladyaccomplice.com>

Dear Hal:

I am not sure if you remember me. I am the American who
was working with you and Mrs. Williamson until I was savaged
by a ferocious emu.

I am writing because I have not heard from you or Mrs.
Williamson for a very long time. I did all the stuff you told me
to do, and then you just dropped off the face of the world.

My feelings were so hurt I decided I did not want anything to
do with you, but then recently, on reflection, I realized that
England is a backward place where they drink hot beer and
have never heard of dental floss, and I figured that maybe the
primitive Internet system over there had been messed up, and
maybe you could not contact me.

If you still need an American to help you with your project, I
am willing to consider it, provided you have a good
explanation for your disappearance.

Steve Hopkins
Hominy Falls, PA

I'm sure they e-mailed me after that, but I am too lazy to
check. I'm busy watching the director's cut DVD of *Dr. Pemberton and His Musical Pants*.

The little yellow car careened crazily as it rolled toward the front gate of the condo complex. Stephie wondered why they drove that way even when they weren't working.

She shrugged. Show people. Go figure.

The car stopped, and Captain Bob was the first one out. Oh God. He was in costume. He walked up to Stephie, raised his pink-and-yellow top hat, and gave her a generous squirt from the plastic daisy on his lapel. Stephie smiled grudgingly and reached for a Kleenex. What she had to put up with to help these folks.

The others began emerging from the car. One, two, three . . . then ten, then twelve, and then a tiny pig with a bow around its neck. Thirteen, fourteen . . .

Good Lord, they were annoying. No wonder people paid good money to toss them.

Nigerians and other 419ers tend to be pretty sickly. The sick ones love to write. Usually, they have esophageal cancer, but sometimes it's breast cancer, and whatever it is, it's invariably fatal. And it "defiles all forms of treatment." They always feel real bad about being schmucks all their lives, and they look for fine foreigners (like you) to help them distribute their money to worthy charities.

Once I told them I was sending the money to a home for old Nazis in Argentina. I said it was a shame, how the Argentineans ignored these "war heroes" and refused to let them march in parades "with their highly decorated units."

I think the best nonprofit I ever came up with was the one that helped indigent midgets.

From: "Mr Crogar Lee" <croleeblahblah@midgetsniffer.net>
To: "stephiehopxxxx" <stephiehopxxxx@yahoo.com>
Subject: Contact Me Asap!

Dear friend,
greetings to you in the name of our heavenly God. This mail might come to you as a surprise and the temptation to ignore it as unserious could come into your mind; but please, consider it a divine wish and accept it with a deep sense of humility. My name is Crogar Lee I'm a 59 years old man. I am British living in Dubai (United Arab Emirate). I was a merchant and owned two businesses in Dubai. I was also married with two children. My wife and two children died in a car accident six years ago. Before this happened my business and concern for making money was all I lived for. I never really cared about other values in life. But since the loss of my family, I have found a new desire to assist helpless families. I have been helping orphans in orphanage/motherless homes. I have donated some money to orphans in Sudan, South Africa, Cameroon, Brazil, Spain, Austria, Germany and some Asian countries. Before I became ill, I kept $4.5 Million in a long-term deposit account in a finance/security company

Presently, I'm in a hospital where I have been undergoing treatment for oesophageal cancer. I have since lost my ability to talk and my doctors have told me that I have only a few months to live. It is my last wish to see this money distributed to charity organizations. Because relatives and friends have plundered so much of my wealth since my illness, I cannot live with the agony of entrusting this huge responsibility to any of them.

Please, I beg you in the name of God to help me collect the deposit and The interest accrued from the company and distributes it amongst charity organizations. your share of will be 30% of the total money for your help and for any cost you incur during the process of collecting and distributing the money to charity organizations.

I,m willing to offer you a reward If you are willing to help; please reply as soon as you can. May the good Lord bless you and your family.

Regards,
Crogar Lee
croleeblahblah@midgetsniffer.net

I know I'm going to catch hell for this from the midget lobby. Maybe I deserve it, but damn it, they send mixed messages. On the one hand, they tell us we have to call them "little people" and take them seriously and not toss them in bars. On the other, they go to work for circuses and let people shoot them out of cannons and juggle them and so on. I wish they'd make up their minds.

Date: Thu, 15 Sep 2005 07:18:49 -0700 (PDT)
From: "Stephanie Hopkins" >stephiehopxxxx@yahoo.com>
Subject: Re: Contact Me Asap!
To: "Mr Crogar Lee" >croleeblahblah@midgetsniffer.net>

Dear Mr. Crogar:

We have a grocery chain called Crogar in the United States, only they spell it "Kroger." Isn't that remarkable? I don't suppose you're related to the people who started it. I went to high school with a boy who was the heir to a grocery fortune. His name was Ralph Foodgiant.

It sounds like your friends and relatives are serious tools. I know what that's like. Last year, my cousin Latrina threw a surprise birthday party for me, and when it was over, she gave me the bill for the cake.

I am very sorry to hear about your illness. I too am a cancer victim. I had a large melanoma on my right baby toe, and the doctors had to take the whole digit, which is now in a jar on my mantel.

As it happens, I am involved with a local charity. I am a volunteer for the Operation Circus Midget Rescue. There are a number of retired circus midgets here in the Sarasota area (home of the Ringling Bros. and Barnum & Bailey Clown College), and they have difficulty finding regular jobs, so OCMR provides them with low-cost housing. We bought up a block of condos with high ceilings and divided them into additional floors, thus doubling the capacity. A four-foot ceiling would be bothersome for you or I, but these folks don't mind it one bit, except for old Bob Talbert who, at five feet three inches, was once billed as "Captain Bob the Giant Midget."

We have received grants from the Mahi Shrine Circus and also from certain celebrities who, while of normal stature, have facial features resembling those of midgets. Just last week we got five hundred dollars from Matt Damon.

I wish I could tell you how it warms my heart when a little beat-up car pulls up outside the manager's office and weary midgets in search of affordable housing start getting out. One after another, until you just can't believe the car could hold that many midgets. I always wonder how they pack them in.

Anyway, let me know what needs to be done, and I will do my best to help.

Stephanie Hopkins
Sarasota, FL

I guess that will also piss off Matt Damon if he ever reads this book. But it's true. There are lots of famous big people who look like they *ought* to be midgets. Randall "Tex" Cobb. Jacqueline Onassis. John C. Reilly. The obnoxious leader of the gang of brats in the *Star Trek* episode where everyone stays a kid forever. You know. The guy who froze to death in *Scrooged*.

What's going on here? I have a theory. These people ARE, in fact, midgets. But they have genes that would make them giants if they didn't also have the midget gene. So what happens is, you get a midget who is also a giant. A giant midget. See what I'm saying? A normal giant is seven or eight feet tall. A giant midget could be as short as five-two.

I'll bet that if Matt Damon didn't have the midget gene, he'd be in the NBA.

My other theory is that these people are midget moles, medically altered to resemble normal people. An international midget conspiracy paid to be stretched by means of hormone therapy and bone surgery, and then they sent them out to infiltrate the rest of civilization. Their mission? To gain power, sponsor political candidates, and pass zoning laws lowering ceiling heights in all new construction.

If we don't stop them, soon we'll all be hunched over and crippled from lower back pain, while they enjoy being able to reach tabletops and counters and cabinet doors for the first time in their lives.

I'm not saying it's true. Just that we need to keep an eye on them.

Date: Thu, 15 Sep 2005 19:41:09 -0400
From: croleeblahblah@midgetsniffer.net
To: "Stephanie Hopkins" <stephiehopxxxx@yahoo.com>
Subject: Thanks

Dear Friend,

First of all I say thank you for taking your limited time out to reply me in this situation that will be of mutual benefit to both of us. This transaction is much free from any risks or troubles, since my money is under the custody of the bank. All these have been properly mapped out to be very hitch free. The only problem i have is for me to present you to the bank as a beneficiary of the money in my account with them since my present predicament cannot make me travel because i need medical attention all the time.

I would hence require the following;

(i) Your full names
(ii)address or the full names and address of your company.
(iv) Your telephone and fax number (iii) Any other personal details or remarks. For easy comunication between us.
Please feel free with all these details because i only need them to identify your as my partners/friend (the beneficiary of my fund). These are very legal procedures that do not go contrary to any international laws.

As soon as you hear from the bank, please inform me immediately, note that you will also help in donating the money to any orphanage home or charity of your choice any where in the world naming me as the donor.

Like I wrote in my first mail to you, your share is 30% from the total sum, for the expected help and assistance in this transaction as i also hope for your understanding.

Let it be known to you that i am a little bit weary, but i have the understanding that friends are discovered and friends are made. I have come to the understanding that I cannot achieve my life long acheivements without trusting someone in this transaction. This brings us to the need for both of us to have absolute trust and believe in one another as we can only fail if we have divided interests. Let trust and honesty be our watchword throughout this transaction.

Best regards,
Lee.

Lee sent me the depressing photo you see below. I'll bet that's really him. I'll bet the dirty bastard snuck into a hospital, went into the room of some poor helpless sick person, dropped trou, stole all the tubes and taped them to himself, and took that picture using a timer.

Outside the frame, the actual patient is turning blue and clawing at the call button.

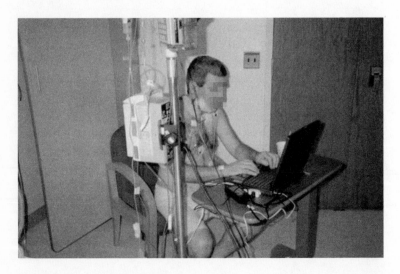

Stephie was deeply moved, and she offered words of encouragement.

Date: Fri, 16 Sep 2005 09:09:45 -0700 (PDT)
From: "Stephanie Hopkins" <stephiehopxxxx@yahoo.com>
Subject: Re: Thanks
To: croleeblahblah@midgetsniffer.net

Dear Mr. Crogar:

The photos you sent are truly heartbreaking. Who is that
person, anyway? If I were him, I would not be buying any
green bananas.

I am attaching a scan of my international passport. I would
appreciate it if you would confirm your identity with a photo,
because I am nervous about doing business with a person
whom I do not know. I would prefer that you pose with a
paper bearing the name of my attorney, Mr. Ron Jeremy.

Here is my contact information:
Stephanie Hopkins
411 Miguelito Loveless Blvd.
Sarasota, FL 34236

I mentioned this project to a few of the midgets, and they
were quite excited. They haven't been this fired up since
Donna Shalala came by and handed out free federal cheese.

I await further instructions.

Stephie

Speaking of midgets and sick people, I have a funny story
about Donna Shalala. I have a source at the University of
Miami who fed me some quasi-reliable gossip about her.
There's a disabled lady in Shalala's building who walks with
crutches. She used to park in the lot right behind the build-

ing, but according to my friend, Shalala banned everyone else from the lot, and now she keeps her chauffeur and limo out there all day, with the motor running. And supposedly the lady with crutches now has to ride a shuttle from a remote lot. I've been on those shuttles. They have three steps.

So, you know. I have no problem with picking on Shalala for being a midget.

Date: Fri, 16 Sep 2005 14:26:45 -0400
From: croleeblahblah@midgetsniffer.net
To: "Stephanie Hopkins" <stephiehopxxxx@yahoo.com>
Subject: Bless You

Dear Stephnie.
Thanks so much your your assistance towards this course of mine. I will forward your details over to the bank making you a beneficiary of my funds with them. When ever you hear from the bank please always inform me so that i can as well monitor the situation.

Like i wrote to you before, my funds with them is four million five hundred thousand american dollars, once they transfer the funds over to you make sure its nothing short of what i have told you. It should be used for charity and orphanage related works, and compensating your self accordinly, you should name you me as the donor so that their prayers will always lead me through.

I truly put my trust in you and it should not be taken for granted. Once they transfer the funds over to you do not betray me do not run away with the money. Hoping to hear from you.

Regards
Lee

"For charity and orphanage related works, *and compensating yourself.*" You don't have to tell ME twice.

I let this loser stew for a while. I love doing that to the ones who claim to have cancer. I get back to them and say things like, "I sure hope you're not dead yet." Then they have to explain why they haven't croaked.

Date: Tue, 20 Sep 2005 10:20:01 -0400
From: croleeblahblah@midgetsniffer.net
To: "Stephanie Hopkins" <stephiehopxxxx@yahoo.com>
Subject: Hello

Dear Stepahie.
How are you doing today? I have long forwarded your details over to my bank. Have you heard from the bank? have they started with the transfer process.

kindly update me please.

lee.

I handed him the usual lie about the bank not getting in touch. And since Lee was pulling at MY heartstrings, I figured it was time for a midget sob story.

Date: Wed, 21 Sep 2005 08:29:41 -0700 (PDT)
From: "Stephanie Hopkins" <stephiehopxxxx@yahoo.com>
Subject: Re: Hello
To: croleeblahblah@midgetsniffer.net

Dear Crowley:

I am so sorry I did not respond to your last e-mail. As you may be aware, we had a hurricane come by here, and it knocked over my baobab tree, which landed on the box that connects the whole neighborhood to the Internet.

I have not heard nothing from no banks. I got a crazy e-mail from a "Lottery Commission" in Botswana, but I do not think that is the same thing.

I will keep an eye out for the bank's e-mail message. I am anxious to receive these funds on behalf of the midgets, as many of them have been reduced to dwelling in storage units, and one has taken refuge in a locker down at the bus station.

Stephie

Boo hoo, boo hoo. Poor little midgets. Crammed into bus station lockers and storage units. And Tupperware containers and abandoned Habitrails.

Date: Sat, 24 Sep 2005 06:52:26 -0400
From: croleeblahblah@midgetsniffer.net
To: "Stephanie Hopkins" <stephiehopxxxx@yahoo.com>
Subject: Hello

Dear Keith.

How are you and how is your weekend as well? Have you heard from thw bank still? or have they contacted you with regards to the transfer process.

Kindly keep me posted on the latest development please.
Regards
Lee

"Keith"? I guess the OxyContin was affecting Lee's thinking. He seemed to have a pretty sturdy tolerance for B.S., so I served him a generous helping.

Date: Sun, 25 Sep 2005 10:22:54 -0700 (PDT)
From: "Stephanie Hopkins" <stephiehopxxxx@yahoo.com>
Subject: Re: Hello
To: croleeblahblah@midgetsniffer.net

Dear Mr. Crowlee:

I believe you may have confused me with another correspondent, as my name is not "Keith." Here in America, Keith is a man's name. I am all woman, although as my age advances, I have had some problems with unwanted hair on my chin and back.

I have not heard a thing from your bank. Perhaps you should give them a call.

I will be unavailable for the next two days, as I and some of my midget friends will be attending a funeral in Louisiana. Some acquaintances of theirs were killed by rising water after a storm. Because of their height, midgets are always the first to drown.

I am going because they need someone to drive the car. They would do it themselves if they could see over the dashboard.

There is one small blessing to be thankful for. Due to the amount of materials involved, their coffins are very inexpensive, and you can put several in one burial plot by arranging them sideways.

Stephie Hopkins
Sarasota, FL

I don't recall whether Lee got back to me after that. I had other midgets to fry.

I know the midgets are going to make my life hell for this. They'll be picketing my house and coming up to me at book signings and butting me in the groin. And eventually I'll end up on midget telethons, telling people I've seen the light and holding hands with Donna Shalala.

After that I'll probably get my ass kicked by Randall "Tex" Cobb.

Library Paste Is Highly Nutritious

Steve sat on the cool linoleum and peered at the concerned faces around him. He felt a wet, sticky, gritty sensation between the fingers of his right hand. And a strange weight on his head, as though he were wearing a skullcap made of mashed potatoes. And what was that refreshing minty smell?

"He seems to be coming out of it," the manager said. "Let's see if we can get him back into his trousers."

I think human beings have a deep-seated need to be truly ruthless once in a while. Take me, for example. Ordinarily, I wouldn't hurt a fly. But put me on a boat out in the Gulf Stream, and I'll happily spend the day jerking helpless fish over the side and bashing their little heads in with an aluminum bat. And then my friends and I will pose for photos, with blood in our hair and guts on our sunglasses. There's something wonderful about having a legal, morally acceptable target for cruelty and insensitivity.

When fish aren't around, thank God I have my spammers.

From: "gwazo daniel" <dannygwazo@slimfast.fr>
Subject: FROM:DANIEL GWAZO
Date: Wed, 14 Dec 2005 11:21:31 +0100

May this mail find you happiness and peace in your life.

I am Daniel Gwazo from Sierre-Leone country. i lost my parent and my late father Dr Rawlings Gwazo made a deposit of money with a bank here in a fixed deposit and the amount is USD15M dollars on a bank here in Abidjan Cote d'Ivoire.

I am presently in Abidjan where the money was been deposited and I have the documents backing up the money at the bank for your claims and our late father told me incase if he died that i should look for someone who has a legitimate bank account abroad to help me claim the money as i am young one, i have the ID Card issued me from the United Nation here in Abidjan Cote D'Ivoire on my arrival as refugess and these will serves you as a proof of who i am.

I believe you as an advanced person that you will not betray the trust we impose on you at the end of the transfer into your personal bank account.

Please we need you to send to me the followings,

1.   your full Name.

2.   Your private phone and fax number

3.   Your banking information

All this i will submit to the bank for the transfer of the money to your bank account which you are going to send.

[SNIP]

Thanks and remaine bless.
Waiting for your reply.
Yours sincerely.
Daniel Gwazo

"Abidjan"? How come African places always sound like they're named after cologne?

I was moved to tears by Danny's plight, so I offered him the best advice I could.

Date: Wed, 14 Dec 2005 09:25:56 -0800 (PST)
From: "Steve H." <xxxx@yahoo.com>
Subject: Re: FROM: DANIEL GWAZO
To: Xxxx dannygwazo@slimfast.fr

Dear Dan:

So sorry to hear about your dad, Mr. Rawlings Gwazlo. I once
had a baseball mitt named Rawlings, and it was very special
to me.

It is unfortunate that you cannot get the bank to release your
fifteen dollars, but I don't see how I can help. Have you talked
to the bank manager? He can probably sort this out for you.

I hope you don't need the money to buy food. You might
consider talking to the folks from Unicef. I assume they have
an office in your area. Generally they donate food to children,
but if you get in the line and hunch down, they probably won't
know the difference.

If you're really in trouble, I can send you a few bucks, but you
better speak up now, because even if I start the ball rolling
now, you could be starving for several more days.

Here's a tip I learned in the Green Berets: when you have no
other resources, grass is edible.

Steve Hopkins
Navel, ID

I think I had a point there. What was the use of all that
maneuvering around, just to get fifteen clams, when he could
be scrunching down in a Unicef line and being showered
with free gruel, candy bars, and probably packages of condoms autographed by Bob Geldof?

Unfortunately, Danny didn't notice that I had gotten the amount wrong, on account of he was kind of a dumbass.

Date: Thu, 15 Dec 2005 10:55:37 +0100 (CET)
From: Xxxx "gwazo daniel" <dannygwazo@slimfast.fr>
Subject: Re: FROM:DANIEL GWAZO
To: "Steve H." <xxxx@yahoo.com>
dear steve,
i thank you for your mail and concern towards my present circumstances as i want you to know that i am currently passing through a very serious and severe times now since i have lost everything in my life as my parents and everything and body is gone, and now i am left with nothing, but sufferings and orphnage as please i will seriouslly need to your help to get the fund transferred as i went to the bank they said that the fund cannot be transferred as i need to get a foreigner to stand as my foreign partner/trustee/guardian to the said fund as it was according to the clause contained in the deposit certificate and agreement entered into between my late father and the bank, above all, i am still not of age.

concerning the unicef, they have a lot of people from different countries, sierra leone, liberia, gabon, burundi etc who are presently seeking refuge in this country and the worst of it all is that this country is presently undergoing an unstable political crisis and they the unicef do not know whom to turn to since in some part of this country there is war.

pls, do respond so that i can advise you on the details of this project proper.

regards,
Daniel

As you will see if you check the dates on my other correspondence, I had about forty million other Nigerians to contend with, so I let Danny drop for a while. I think there's something inherently funny about stalling a guy who claims he's dying of starvation. But I finally responded, and as always, I had a good explanation.

Date: Tue, 10 Jan 2006 09:01:23 -0800 (PST)
From: "Steve H." <xxxx@yahoo.com>
Subject: Re: FROM:DANIEL GWAZO
To: Xxxx "gwazo daniel" <dannygwazo@slimfast.fr>

Dear Dan-O:

So very sorry to wait so long before replying. I hope you will forgive me. I neglected to take my medication, and I am afraid I had one of my spells. They found me sitting on the floor at Office Depot, singing "Drill ye Tarriers Drill" and eating library paste. I am much better now however.

I don't know if you know this, but paste-eating has become such a problem here in the US, the government now requires the manufacturers to meet basic nutritional requirements. A pound of this stuff will keep you alive for several days. And it has a nice minty flavor. However, they haven't done much to improve the taste of copier toner.

Please tell me you are still alive so I can help you.

You know you have sunk pretty low when you find yourself trying to steal money from a paste-eater. By the way, I have no idea whether paste is nutritious or not, or even if it's poisonous. So don't run to Office Depot and tell them you want a quart of paste and a spoon because Steve said it was scrumptious.

I think if I ever have to babysit a really obnoxious kid, I'll hand him some of this stuff and go, "Kids in Abidjan would give their right arm for a nice can of paste."

Date: Wed, 11 Jan 2006 17:05:12 +0100 (CET)
From: Xxxx "gwazo daniel" <dannygwazo@slimfast.fr>
Subject: Re: FROM:DANIEL GWAZO
To: "Steve H." <xxxx@yahoo.com>

dear steve h,

thanks for your mail and sorry for the tradgic inccident that happened to you as i thank God you are ok and well now.

for me, i am still alife and waiting to hearing from you.

pls, do respond immediately.

regards,
Daniel

Yes, Danny, I was one of the lucky ones. It just so happens that Miami's Jackson Memorial Hospital is the world's foremost research facility in the field of paste addiction. It was touch and go for a while. But after two days of treatment, I finally passed an enormous collage.

I was alarmed to see that even after receiving my e-mail, Danny was still waiting to hear from me.

Date: Wed, 11 Jan 2006 10:03:11 -0800 (PST)
From: "Steve H." <xxxx@yahoo.com>
Subject: Re: FROM:DANIEL GWAZO
To: Xxxx "gwazo daniel" <dannygwazo@slimfast.fr>

Dear Danny:

I am here to let you know that you are now hearing from me. I will try to help you with your starvation problem. However. I do not see how getting fifteen dollars released will be of much assistance. Fifteen dollars is not much money. Maybe a dollar goes farther in Africa. I keep seeing commercials saying I can feed a dirty orphan for forty cents a month. Honestly, I am inclined to simply wire you five bucks or even just put a "care package" in the mail to you. Do you like Nabisco Easy Cheese? It comes in a pressurized can and lasts for months or even years, and you can even use it as bathtub caulk or a fragrant, attention-getting hairdressing. I could send you a box, along with some clam chowder and goldfish crackers.

I'll do whatever you want me to do. I think you ought to be out looking for a job, though. Do they have McDonald's restaurants in your country? They are always looking for presentable counter help.

I am unclear on your location. You mention Sergio Leone. Isn't he a film director?

Steve Hopkins
Navel, ID

I can't believe I blasphemed the name of Sergio Leone like that. I'm glad Eli Wallach isn't alive to read this. Wait— maybe he is. Yes, I just checked Imdb.com. That's nice. Jack Elam, however, is as dead as a post.

If you think Danny's e-mails have been sad up to this point, wait until you read the next one.

Date: Thu, 12 Jan 2006 12:04:49 +0100 (CET)
From: Xxxx "gwazo daniel" <dannygwazo@slimfast.fr>
Subject: Re: FROM:DANIEL GWAZO
To: "Steve H." <xxxx@yahoo.com>
sir,
thanks for your mail.
the money in question is usd15m and not usd15.
there is no mcdonald's here.

pls, help me out as i am from sierra leone and now in cote d'ivoire because of the war in mty country and now in the refuge camp

Can that possibly be true? A whole country without a McDonald's? Can you imagine getting up on Saturday morning and not being able to purchase an Egg McMuffin?

Danny's situation was sad. He had been starving for what, a month now? The poor kid probably looked like Lara Flynn Boyle. Thank God ONE of us was getting some decent grub. I figured it would do him good to read about it.

Date: Mon, 30 Jan 2006 07:32:13 -0800 (PST)
From: "Steve H." <xxxx@yahoo.com>
Subject: Re: FROM: DANIEL GWAZO
To: Xxxx "gwazo daniel" <dannygwazo@slimfast.fr>

Dear Danny:

Sorry I didn't get back to you sooner about your starvation thing. I have been at a health spa for people who have trouble putting on weight. I am cursed with a high metabolism, so I have to make myself eat. For the last two weeks, I've been stuffing myself with steaks, mashed potatoes with gravy and butter, cheesecake, ice cream, and so on. And I had to drink beer all day. I managed to put on four pounds. I'm sure you will be very happy for me.

Anyway, tell me what I can do to help you. Would a box of Snickers bars help you? I have a bunch of them. I eat about seven a day. I'm having one right now, sliced into a bowl of Jell-O pudding.

I am sorry to hear they don't have McDonald's over there. But Wendy's is better anyway, wouldn't you agree? I may go there later.

I must close now. On orders from my doctor, at about this time every day, I have to eat a whole pie.

Steve Hopkins
Navel, ID

I know. You think that's the meanest thing you ever read. That's because you haven't seen my correspondence with perennial cancer victim Ahmed Saeed. *"Please, please accept my apology for making you wait. Thank you for remaining alive." "I have contacted Mr. Carrington again and instructed him to work this matter out with you. Please make haste, because as you have noted, soon you will be dead."*

I guess hunger was ruining Danny's mood. You know how it is. A few weeks without food, and some guys get all pissy.

Date: Thu, 2 Feb 2006 11:15:16 +0100 (CET)
From: Xxxx "gwazo daniel" <dannygwazo@slimfast.fr>
Subject: Re: FROM:DANIEL GWAZO
To: "Steve H." <xxxx@yahoo.com>

Dear Steve H,

please sir am not here for jokes if you went to be serious be or forget about my problem you are not God.

Bye.
Daniel

I was surprised to learn that I wasn't God. That explains why I didn't do better on the SAT.

It hurt, being pushed away like that. I was trying to give Danny hope, by eating nine steaks and seven servings of

cheesecake every day, and this is the reward I got for my sac-
rifice. But I wasn't bitter. Pettiness just isn't in my nature.

Date: Thu, 2 Feb 2006 09:12:26 -0800 (PST)
From: "Steve H." <xxxx@yahoo.com>
Subject: Re: FROM:DANIEL GWAZO
To: Xxxx "gwazo daniel" <dannygwazo@slimfast.fr>

Dear Danny:

This is a fine how-do-you-do. I was anxious to help you on
account of you are starving, and you respond with this nasty
message. I can only assume it is the hunger talking. That
reminds me, it's almost time for my cheesecake facial.

I hope you will be all right. Remarkably, I just received a
similar appeal from another gentleman who says he is also in
Tea Leoni. I am in the process of sending him a couple of
hundred dollars for malaria drugs and some special leprosy
soap.

Good luck, my brave little accidental Olsen twin. Let me know
if you ever get state-side, and I will take you to Sonic.

A lot of guys would have given Danny a righteous ream-
ing, but not me. I can honestly say that if I ever ran into him
here in America, I would shake his hand, embrace him as a
brother, and offer him half of my paste sandwich.

***********Chuku Peter, the Prostate Gland,*********** and the Pin-Setting Machine

Steve stared at the mirror and daubed at his neck with a sterile wipe. He could not believe his eyes.

"Harley-Davison?" he sputtered. "Harley-DAVISON?"

"Geez, I'm sorry," said Clem, "I guess I wasn't concentrating. Tell you what. How about if I give you a discount next time?"

Steve glared at him. He said, "By hell, if I still had feet, I'd break one off in your sorry ass."

I guess I should start by telling you about Sithole Baloy. I think that's the best way to attack the spaghetti-like knot of Nigerian e-mails that lead up to the saga of Chuku Peter. I have so many aliases, and I corresponded with so many people, and I involved them with each other so much, it will never be possible to present this stuff in a logical, comprehensible manner. Be content to laugh and enjoy it, because you will never make sense of it.

A long time ago, a guy calling himself "Sithole Baloy" sent me an e-mail, and I ended up tormenting him for a while. I called him "Baldy Sh_thole" and referred to his sick mother as "Mother Sh_thole." He finally ran off, but not before another spammer referred to him as "Baldy's Sh_thole" and claimed to be his business partner.

The next time I heard from Baldy, he had completely forgotten who I was. If it was really him. For all I know, half the spammers in Africa use Sithole Baloy as an alias.

Anyway, I got an e-mail purporting to be from "Chuku Peter," and it was cc'd to sitholebaloy1@dungheap.net. For some reason, these guys tend to cc themselves. This one went to my Steve Hopkins address.

Date: Wed, 23 Mar 2005 16:12:56 +0100
From: chukupetercottontail@goofmail.com.br
Subject: URGENT REPLY
To: sitholebaloy1@dungheap.net

Dear Sir,

REQUEST FOR YOUR UNRESERVED ASSISTANCE

Firstly, I must solicit your confidence in this transaction, this is by virtue of its nature as being utterly confidential and top secret. Though I know that a transaction of this magnitude will make any one apprehensive and worried, but I am assuring you that all will be well at the end of the day . . .

Let me start by first introducing myself properly to you. I am Chuku Peter, a Manager at the Union Bank of Nigeria PLC, Lagos Nigeria . . .

A foreigner, Mr. Michael, an oil Merchant/contractor with the federal Government of Nigeria, until his death three years ago in a ghastly air crash including his immediate Family, banked with us here at the Union Bank of Nigeria PLC, Lagos Nigeria, and had a closing balance of USD$25M (Twenty Five Million United States Dollars) which the bank now unquestionably expects to be claimed by any of his available foreign next of kin or alternatively be donated to a discredited trust fund for arms and ammunition at a military war collage here in Nigeria.

Fervent valuable efforts had been made by this bank to get in touch with any his next of kin, or Foreign Family relative (as *his wife and only Daughter died along side with him in the Plane Crash), but all our efforts prooved abortive . . .*

Thank you in advance for your anticipated co-operation.

Regards. MR. Chuku Peter

You can only imagine how relieved I was to be reunited with Baldy.

Dear Chuck:

I am gasping with excitement! God has smiled on me at last! My wife left me for my own sister. I was fired from Denny's for adjusting myself while a customer was looking. I went bowling, got caught in the pin-setting machine, and lost both feet and my prostate gland. But finally I have a way out! Can it really be true? Can it?

I understand the need for secrecy. I suggest we communicate in code. I know a very simple code I can teach you. Look: "Igerianay isway ethay eekingray armpitway ofway Africaway." That means, "Nigeria is a lovely country which exports palladium."

I can't believe your friend Mr. Micheal's plane crashed into your bank! I hope you weren't hurt! I don't understand the part about giving his dead daughter an abortion, but then I have no formal medical training.

I agree that it is ridiculous to donate his fortune to a war collage. I think collages are stupid. And how much can a few old magazines and some glue cost? Not twenty-five million dollars. That is for sure.

I have not felt this hopeful since I found myself watching the paramedics striving valiantly to free my prostate gland from the pin-setting machine. I hope this time I will not be as bitterly disappointed.

1. Steve Horatio Hopkins
2. Telephone: 305-xxx-xxxx
3. Fax: 202-xxx-xxxx [fax line for a political organization that I find annoying]

Steve Hopkins
Plankton, ME

I honestly wonder if this was the same guy. E-mail crooks deal with hundreds of stupid American victims. I guess it's possible that he simply forgot me. Or maybe it was another guy. Who cares? It wasn't long before he sent me his answer.

Date: Mon, 28 Mar 2005 07:46:52 -0800 (PST)
From: "chuku peter" <chukupeterbutthead@yahoo.com>
Subject: Details.
To: "Steve H." <xxx@yahoo.com>

Dear Steve,

I am very grateful for the response that you have given to my message. I commend your effort to have summoned the courage to write and indicate your unflinching support for this deal. Practically this is a deal, which I personally want to solicit your assistance to execute for the mutual benefit of both of us. I did not send this message to any other person bearing your name neither did I conceive this Idea for deceipt . . .

What we need to do in order to claim these Funds from the Bank is to have you present yourselve as the original Next of Kin to the Late Mr. Michael Jean Hopkins. You are to claim that

the family had awarded your relatives financial estate to you
and based on that, you are calling on the Bank to repatriate
the Funds to you for your use . . .

This is not a game and if you feel that it is a game I will advise
you to inform me of your indecision now and we shall forget
it all . . .

Thank you for the anticipated support.

Chuku Peter.

Steve was anxious to help, despite his horrible disabilities.
And he wanted to bring his sister Stephanie in on the deal.

Date: Mon, 28 Mar 2005 10:12:38 -0800 (PST)
From: "Steve H." <xxx@yahoo.com>
Subject: Re: Details.
To: "chuku peter" <chukupeterbutthead@yahoo.com>

Dear Chuck:

God, this is exciting! I can't wait to take part!

Incidentally, if there are any expenses that need to be
handled, I am well able to cover them, as I successfully sued
the bowling alley and the manufacturer of the shoes that
caused me to slide under the pin-setting machine. Also, the
people who made the floor wax. That stuff is slicker than snot
on a doorknob.

I e-mailed my dear sister Stephanie about it. She is as
delighted as I am. Please, please forgive me for telling her.
She has been my rock through all my troubles, and I would
trust her with my life.

If you are determined to keep 50% of the proceeds, I guess I cannot stop you, but it seems crazy, given that African countries nationalize their banks about as often as a fat baby farts.

Let me know what has to be done.

Steve Hopkins
Plankton, ME

Stephanie . . . oh, that Stephanie. She was Steve's angel of mercy. She was the one whose steadfast love and support helped him get through those trying first few months, as he learned to get by without feet or a prostate gland. Steve trusted her implicitly. Be that as it may, as soon as she got the e-mail, she tried to shaft him.

Dear Chuck:

I am Steve Hopkins's sister, Stephanie. He was so excited, he forwarded this e-mail to me.

I hate to be disloyal to my own brother, but I think you should consider dealing with me instead. Steve is a fine person, but he is sure to blow this deal. For one thing, he is only able to receive mail at the Plankton Institute for the Mentally Unstable. That will be a red flag to the bank. As you know from his e-mail, he lost both feet and his prostate gland in a bowling accident, and ever since, he has spent the better part of the day crying and—for some reason I cannot fathom—placing orders at websites selling expensive shoes.

In addition to this, I must inform you that he has a large unsightly goiter, which he has decorated with a tattoo of a Harley-Davidson insignia.

I on the other hand am a sophisticated woman whose figure defies her seventy-four years. I am willing to send a photo as proof.

Let me suggest that you continue dealing with Steve as though everything were all right. He has a large amount of capital because he successfully sued the bowling alley. If there are any expenses involved, let him handle them. This will save us both money. Then when the time is right, I will step in and finish the deal in his place. There is little he can do, as he is allowed to leave the institute only on Christmas and of course, Anne B. Davis's birthday. In case you don't know, Miss Davis was our Secretary of Defense during the Franco-American war, and she also invented the cotton gin.

I will make things right with Steve once the cash is in hand. Perhaps I will surprise him with a pair of crocodile shoes.

Stephanie Hopkins
Plankton, ME

"Chuck" did not go out of his way to make me aware that my sister was planning on screwing me over, although he did let a few details slip in his next e-mail.

Date: Tue, 29 Mar 2005 06:12:27 -0800 (PST)
From: "chuku peter" <chukupeterbutthead@yahoo.com>
Subject: Details.
To: "Steve H." <xxx@yahoo.com>

Dear Steve,

I have just sent to you a Text Format Copy of an Application for the Repatriation of the Funds.

I will advise you to let you and your sister run the deal. I will take 30%, Your Sister will be entitled to 30%, while you will have 30% also. Then for your expences you will take the remaining 10% to off-set your expences.

Fill the Letter while re-typing or you may allow your Sister to use her personal Bank Information for this purpose while we claim the Funds.

After you must re-typed the Letter, I will want you to send it to me first before sending to the Bank. The Letter must be signed by you or your Sister:

I am waiting for your responce confirmation to this effect.

Regards,

Chuku.

Steve was perplexed. He hadn't invited Stephanie to join in the profits. Also, he had received an e-mail from a spammer named Kentas Anderson, and he wanted Chuck's take on it.

Date: Tue, 29 Mar 2005 10:19:33 -0800 (PST)
From: "Steve H." <xxx@yahoo.com>
Subject: Re: Details.
To: "chuku peter" <chukupeterbutthead@yahoo.com>
Dear Chuck:
I am very confused. How did my sister get involved in this? All I did was tell her about it. I asked her if she knew what you were talking about, but she said she has not had any contact with you.

I love my sister, but I do not see why she should get any of my money! Also, some nut named Anderson sent me an

e-mail claiming he is the only Nigerian I should deal with and that you are trying to swindle me. I will forward his e-mail to you so you can tell me what his problem is.

I guess I should explain about Kentas Anderson. He's a real spammer. Right after I received Chuck's latest e-mail, he sent me this gem. Steve and Stephie both received it.

Date: Tue, 29 Mar 2005 11:41:52 +0100
From: "kentas anderson" <prvrt_kentas@rupaul.pt>
To:
Subject: WHAT YOU SHOULD KNOW ABOUT YOUR FUND

FROM THE DATABSE DEPT,
CENTRAL BANK OF NIGERIA (C.B.N)
ABUJA, HEADQUATERS.
NIGERIA,

RE- WHAT YOU SHOULD KNOW ABOUT YOUR FUND

ATTENTION,

Listen and listen good.

Keep this mail and information very confidential.

I am the current Information and Database analyst of the Treasury/Payment Investigation Department of the Central Bank of Nigeria.

I'm contacting you to stop you from any further contact phone or email with anybody whatsoever, be it an attorney, bank Manager or anyother person here in Nigeria.

I was inaugurated into this post as the new database analyst on the 10th of January, 2005. As I was going through several out-going payment files handed over to me by the past government, I discovered a lot of undue finanacial irregularities and confusions in your payment file with treasury dept of CBN.

Your payment file is currently with CENTRAL BANK OF NIGERIA and no longer in the bank where it was initially deposited. Your file with me here is completely mutilated by those who claimed to be helping you get your fund transfered to your account in your country. I really feel for you and I cannot just fold my arms and watch your fund go this way here simply because you are not here to help yourself.

Therefore, I've withdrawn my submission paper for conversion of the funds to CBN Treasury which I was mandated to do with immediate effect.

Several payments files have suffered this type of financial irregularities and uptill now, the fund are rendered unservicable for the owner.

I have already made up my mind to help you so long as you stop all further communicatio with everyother person and listen to me with rapt attention. Those you are currently dealing with have the intention of using your name to claim your fund to their own selfish interest and that is why you must completely stop dealing with them from now on otherwise you will end up loosing your legal fund. I have the whole data with me here.

My position makes it very possible for all arrangement that would peacefully ensure the transfer of the fund to your account to be well perfected. I will help you to enure that your Fund is transfered directly to your account in your country without openning any account here.

But then, you must agree to the following terms and conditions of mine before we proceed:

[IRRELEVANT STUFF OMITTED—THIS GUY NEVER SHUTS UP]

A stitch in time they say saves nine. This is the only reliable channel for you otherwise all other efforts MUST be in vain.

I look forward to hearing from you. I'll attach in a seperate e-mail my photo, work ID double faces for your reference as soon as I hear from you.

Regards

Engr. Kentas Anderson
INFORMATION TECH & DATA ANALYST TREASURY
PAYMENT INVESTIGATION DEPT
CBN

I smelled an opportunity to pit two spammers against each other, so I forwarded that mess to Chuck. And then I created my own Chuku Peter address. I forwarded the Anderson message to my Chuku Peter address from Stephie, with this note:

Dearest Chuck:

Thanks again for the lovely photo of you at the beach! I would tell you my thoughts, but they are so naughty . . . and I so want you to think of me as a proper lady.

Chuck, I am forwarding a disturbing e-mail from a person who says I am to stop all my dealings with Nigerians other than himself. He claims I am being swindled! Surely he cannot be talking about you. You are my angel man and my chocolate fantasy.

By the way, my idiot brother doesn't suspect a thing. And I am afraid he is having little success with his new prosthetic feet.

Your adoring Stephie
Plankton, ME

Meanwhile, Stephie gave Kentas a piece of her mind. And yes, I DO know how to spell "Michael."

Dear Mr. Anderson:

How dare you tell me not to contact anyone else from Nigeria!

I am currently working with the fine Nigerian barrister Chuck Peters on a very important financial matter. My relative Micheal Hopkins was on a plane, and it crashed into Mr. Peters's bank, and Mr. Peters is helping me to recover Micheal's money by various and sundry modalities.

Are you trying to tell me Chuck Peters, a fine upstanding Nigerian barrister, cannot be trusted? I will have you know that he sent me a picture of his passport, as well as a marvelous photo of himself in a bathing suit.

If you know something about Mr. Peters that I don't, I would like to know what it is, because he seems to be a fine compassionate man and he has beautiful calves.

Stephanie Hopkins
Plankton, ME

I sent the following message from my Chuck address to the real Kentas:

MR. ANDERSON YOU STUPID BASTARD:

MY GOOD AMERICAN FRIEND STEPHANIE HOPKINS INFORMS ME THAT YOU HAVE HAD THE CHEEK TO CONTACT HER AND DEMAND THAT SHE STOP DOING BUSINESS WITH ME BY ALL MODALITIES. I AM QUITE INCENSED AT YOU AND WOULD LIKE TO KNOW THE MEANING OF YOUR INTERFERENCE.

I HAVE WORKED VERY HARD TO CONVINCE THIS SILLY WOMAN THAT I AM A TRUSTWORTHY BARRISTER SOON TO SEND HER A CHECK FOR SEVERAL MILLIONS OF DOLLARS, AND I HAVE ALREADY OBTAINED OVER 1000 USD FROM HER.

IF YOU DO NOT DESIST FROM ALL COMMUNICATIONS WITH HER I SHALL FIND YOU AND GIVE YOU A DAMNED GOOD THRASHING.

CHUKU PETER

Naturally, the real Kentas Anderson fell for it and sent Stephie this e-mail:

Dear Stephie,
How are you today?
I want you to understand that the information I sent to you is binding whether you like it or not. Without me assistance you will never have acess to your fund here. Anybody promising you any help is only decieving you including your so called Chuck. He want to use your name to claim your fund. Be careful.
Engr.Kentas

I thought Chuck should be very angry about that, so I sent Anderson another e-mail from his phony address, with the subject line "YOU GODDAMN BASTARD."

ANDERSON I DEMAND TO KNOW WHY YOU ARE PESTERING MY AMERICAN BUSINESS CONTACTS! THIS IS THE SECOND DAMNED TIME IN ONE DAY YOU HAVE MOLESTED MY CLIENTELES! FIRST YOU TELL MS. STEPHANIE HOPKINS TO DESIST ACTIVITIES WITH ME AND THAT I AM A SCOUNDREL, AND NOW YOU ARE EMAILING HER LUNATIC BROTHER AS WELL!

IF I FIND YOU I SHALL JOLLY WELL BASH YOUR FACE IN. LEAVE THESE PEOPLE ALONE AND FIND YOUR OWN CONTACTS.

I HAVE TOLD BOTH OF MY CONTACTS THAT YOU ARE IN PRISON FOR BREAKING INTO WOMEN'S HOMES AND STEALING THEIR UNDERGARMENTS. HOW DO YOU LIKE THAT, YOU MISERABLE CUR?

CHUKU PETER

I know it's confusing. It confuses me, too. Don't worry about it. There is not going to be a test.

I had my phony Chuku Peter address send Stephie and Steve a comforting e-mail, telling them to pay no attention to Kentas. They both received the same text, only Steve's version lacked the part about the sarong.

Dear Stephanie:

Please have no more dealings with the disreputable rascal Mr. Kentas Anderson. He is a most foolish man and a person of no consequence. In fact, he is in prison here in Lagos. He broke into the home of a wealthy woman and the polices caught him modeling her underclothes and smearing himself with currant jam. It is quite comical, really.

Pay this fool no mind and let us continue with our fine enterprise.

Thank you again for the photo. You look quite lovely in your new sarong.

Chuku Peter
Barrister

Why send a stupid lying e-mail to myself? So I could forward it to Kentas, naturally. Chuku (me) sent it to Kentas (real) under the heading, "KENTAS ANDERSON THE FILTHY PERVERT," and he added this note:

ANDERSON, YOU DISGUSTING MAN:

SEE THE EMAIL I HAVE SENT TO MY AMERICAN CONTACTS ABOUT YOU. THEY NOW BELIEVE YOU ARE A CRIMINAL WHODRESSES IN WOMEN'S UNDERTHINGS. GOOD LUCK TRYING TO STEAL THEM AWAY FROM ME NOW!

Here is where Kentas blew it. He sent Stephie a defensive e-mail, and he stupidly attached his photo, as well as a shot of his phony Nigerian ID. Now I had pictures to play with.

Dear Stephanie,

Thanks again for writing. How are you today? Just like I was trying to explain to you yesterday, the guy Chuck is only trying to blackmail my name.

He has seen that I'm out to block his way. His plan is to decieve you. He is already working with somebody to claim your money for their own selfish interest. I contacted you so that I can stop them from perfecting the arragement against you.

I'm an onnocent, honest man as you can see in my photo, and work Id CARDS which I'm sending to you.

Without me, all your work and efforts with him must be in total vain because your payment file is already on my desk.

Contact me asap so that I can help you.

I'm attaching all my prevate details for your reference.

Regards,

Engr.Kentas Anderson

Really bad move, attaching those files. I cranked up Photoshop, and within a few minutes, I had a wonderful item to send back to Kentas. I even gave him a decidedly metrosexual smirk.

Dear Kentas:

I do not know what to believe. I sent Chuck the ID card photo you sent me, and I told him it looked like you were telling the truth. He sent me back a very disturbing photo, which I am attaching. He claims you altered this photo, and that the police make you carry this card as proof of your curious tendencies.

I really wanted to collect that money, but I am so confused, I think I'm just going to forget all about it. My heart is absolutely broken, but I just do not know whom to trust.

If this photo is real, you should just acknowledge what you are and learn to celebrate it. Folks like you are treated well here in the U.S., and they even march in colorful parades.

Stephanie Hopkins
Plankton, ME

Kentas was not amused at ALL.

Dear Stephenie,

How are you today? Your friend Chucks ie treathening my life here simply because I told you the simple truth in which him and his group are planning to use your name to claim your fund.

All the information I gave you about myself are duly subject to further verifications as the case maybe.

For the last time, I'm writing to let you know that from now hence forth, I'm withdrawing my self from helping you since you has made it a habit forwarding my personal mails to you to the idiot.

Maybe after wasting your time with him, you may come back to me, but that would depends whether I would be free to help you then. If you really desire my help, then you must stop contact with Chucks otherwise stop writing me.

Regards,

Kentas

You're lost, right? Well, it gets worse. I thought it would be funny to add some more characters. I logged into my fake Chuck Peters account and sent Kentas this message:

Mr. Anderson:

I have learned that my 10-year-old daughter Effiwat has been using my work computer to send you insulting emails, posing as a man named Chuku Peterson. She has also involved herself with a criminal enterprise, attempting to extract monies from foolish Americans. I am quite incensed at her. I have taken the situation in hand and given her a good dose of the belt. Please accept my apologies. I hope she did not frighten you.

I prefer not to state my name.

Stephie was fed up with Kentas, so she laid into him.

Dear Kentas:

I think I finally know whom to believe.

Chuck would never threaten anyone. In addition to his duties as a barrister, he informs me that he is a minister of the gospel. A clergyman like Chuck would never stoop to employing violence. You, on the other hand, are a strange man who prances around in a brassiere and is forced to carry a government card identifying himself as a pervert.

Chuck says you are a disintegritable nancy boy.

I have sent Chuck $1,500 to get our business venture going because I believe he is a fine man as well as having beautiful brown eyes and a marvelous physique.

I am quite hurt that you would try to deceive me like this. Go find yourself another victim and for the love of God, stop stealing people's lingerie.

Stephie Hopkins
Plankton, ME

Kentas did not know what to make of the message from Effiwat's mom. By the way, "Effiwat" is a real name. I found it on a list of African baby names.

Here is what Kentas had to say to Effi:

Dear,

I cannot understand you.

Effi had recovered from her spanking, and she was determined not to let her mother screw up a good thing. She got back to Kentas, under the subject line "THE HOPKINS MATTER":

PAY NO ATTENTION TO THE PREVIOUS EMAIL IT WAS SENT BY AN UNRELIABLE PERSON WHO BROKE INTO MY OFFICES TO STEAL WHISKY.

IT IS LAUGHABLE THAT YOU WOULD THINK I AM A TEN YEAR OLD GIRL. THAT IS UTTER BOLLOCKS. I AM A LARGE MAN WEIGHING OVER THIRTEEN STONE AND IF YOU DO NOT STOP BOTHERING MY STUPID AMERICAN FRIENDS AND MEDDLING IN MY BUSINESS I SHALL STOP YOU BY WHATEVER MODALITIES NECESSARY.

Respond to chukupeterbutthead@yahoo.com [Chuku's real e-mail address]

Unfortunately, I no longer have the ensuing e-mails in which Effi's mom tried to start a romantic relationship with Kentas. However, I do have Chuck's cautionary e-mail to Steve. Unbelievably, he turned on Stephie.

Dear Steve,

Pardon me for not explaining to you that you may receive such an Information. I want you to know that the death of Mr. Michael Hopkins, has been publicised and, that gives a whole ample opportunity to some other government officials to have this Information and, as such may use it to deceive people that are Innocent. To start with, you have to remember that it is your Bank Account Information we are going to use for the Repatriation.

Also, I want you to know that I cannot do this deal alone. This is the reason why I have emplored your assistance in this deal. So you should not give any not even part of the Information to this Anderson Fellow, because he is seeking to find out from you what the bases of our deal is all about. There and then he will strike with his colleagues as they will hijack the deal from you and I.

On the issue of your Sister, I never wanted you to inform anyone about this deal but, to my surprise you informed your sister about the deal. The Truth is that I am in agreement with her since you are disabled. She can front in your place but, you are going to provide the Bank Account Information where the funds shall be remitted into. We can do this with her since you have already informed her.

She wrote to me asking for this to be done with her. But, I cannot betray you since you were the first person I had contacted for this deal. We do not have much time. If you are truelly interested and, you want us to do this you must be prepared to see more of such Messages from people like Anderson. Never mind them because if you should follow my advise, they will never ruin our plans.

I will forward to you the message your sister sent to me for you to know that I am been frank and, honest with you and your sister. I will never cheat on you people. Do co-operate with me so that we can have this deal sealed perfectly well.

Thank you for the understanding.

Regards,

Chuku.

I guess spammers have a code after all. Steve was comforted by Chuck's message, and he wanted to do everything he could to move things along. Even though he was struggling to get used to his new mechanical feet.

Dear Chuck:

I apologize wholeheartedly for not getting back to you sooner. They have been trying to fix my foot problem with some prosthetics, and it has been a grueling week of physical therapy for me. I managed to do okay on the walking

exercises, but many adjustments will have to be made before I can resume line-dancing. That is my passion.

I have total faith in my physician, Dr. Detroit.

If Stephanie went behind my back, it is only because she cares about me and wants the best for me. I wish she had told me first, but she was probably concerned that the exertion would be too much for me.

As for Anderson, she informs me—perhaps you can corroborate this—that he is a criminal who breaks into people's homes in Nigeria and takes women's clothing for his own use. Can you believe that? Like you, she says basically that he is a dirty son of a bitch. Excuse my language.

Get back to me on Monday and tell me what we need to do.

Steve Hopkins

If you ever decide to torture Nigerians for yourself, one great tactic is to ask them over and over again what they want you to do. You can usually extend the process by two or three weeks that way. Chuck was still holding on, and his next e-mail introduced me to a wonderful Nigerian slang term.

Dear Hopkins,

I have already told you what to do. I sent to you a Letter of application which was in the form of a Text Format. You are supposed to re-type the Letter and fill the Information required and, send to the Bank. But, before sending the Letter, you are to send it to me for review.

Thank you for the co-operation. Your Sister, may be playing games on me but, I refused to become such a nitch.

Thanks you once again.

Regards,
Chuku.

I cackled helplessly when I saw the word "nitch." I still have no idea what it means. But I was tired of Chuck, so I decided to send him a message by incorporating "nitch" in one of my songs. As is so often the case, I looked to *The Flintstones* for inspiration. I love writing parodies of rock and roll's hit tune, "The Twitch."

Dear Chuck:

I am too distressed to go on. The bad blood between you and my imaginary sister, combined with the stress of adapting to my new Rubbermaid feet, has spoiled my enthusiasm. Also, the tension has inflamed my goiter, forcing me to wear a chin sling made from a converted jockstrap.

I wish you luck in your endeavors, and I leave you with a song. I did not have time to write an original tune, so I borrowed the one from the famous hipster anthem "The Twitch."

Yahoo address, cheap PC,
Sending spam to you and me,
Sitting on the caps lock key,
Employing all modalities.
Yeah, yeah, yeah, yeah, yeah, yeah, yeah!
We're gonna NITCH!

There's a town I know where the mugus go called LAGOS!
Nitch, nitch!
When they get an itch to be a nitch in Lagos!
It's a nitchin' town so I'll see you down in Lagos!
Nitch, nitch!

Well, we'll nitch around the goats tonight in Lagos!
Nitch, nitch!
And Chuck is gonna spam with all his might in Lagos!
Nitch, nitch!
It's a nitchin' town, so I'll see ya down in Lagos!
Nitch, nitch!
Yeah the nitchin's fine, have yourself a time in Lagos!

P.S. Stephie sends her love and says she wants to have 1,000 of your babies.

Steve Hopkins
Plankton, ME

I also felt that Stephie should bid Chuck a proper farewell. I had her compose a note to him, and I attached the photo she made for Afolabi. Remember? The topless shot with Afolabi's face on each nipple?

Dear Chuck:

I am sorry you think I am such a bitch. Or nitch, as the case may be. I wish we could have gotten to know each other better. Farewell, my love. I hope that from time to time, you will look at the attached photo of me and remember me with fondness and no small degree of arousal.

I made it for another African boyfriend, Olademeji Afolabi, but as far as I can tell, Nigerians are one hundred percent fungible.

Stephanie Hopkins
Plankton, ME

Chuck finally got the message and moved on. Kentas Anderson went on to become an exotic dancer. And Steve Hopkins is still trying to get the hang of those Rubbermaid feet.

***********The Wrath of a Shemale Scorned***********

Kentas sat in the heat of his shack in Soweto, thumbing through an old copy of Vogue *and dabbing at his eyes with a bit of crumpled Kleenex. His latest e-mail venture had gone sour, he had broken a heel on his best pumps, and the tape beneath his dress had given way during some heavy petting with an unsuspecting gentleman friend.*

Adolf had really had him going. "Herr Anderson," he had always begun. So . . . so continental. So courtly. Kentas had really felt that he could trust him. "Lederhosen," indeed. Adolf and his buddies were probably having a pretty good laugh, at their walled compound outside Buenos Aires.

Kentas Anderson, Registered Pervert, continued spamming people after our first encounter. He kept sending out the same lame e-mail about how he was the only trustworthy African spammer. One day my crazy new alias received it.

Fecha: Tue, 10 Jan 2006 16:45:44 +0200 (EET)
Asunto: Mail
De: "kentas378" <kentas378@mypanties.com>

Dear,
Listen and listen good.
Keep this mail and information very confidential.

[SNIP]

I therefore contacted you on trust and with complete confidence that you should as a matter of utmost importance,

STOP any further contact with anybody, person or group including your so-called representing attorney because apart from me, no other person can help you get the fund transfered to your account in your country.

[SNIP]

A stitch in time they say saves nine. This is the only reliable channel for you otherwise all other efforts MUST be in vain.

I will send my personal details to you once I hear directly from you.

ENGR.KENTAS ANDERSON
INFORMATION TECH & DATA ANALYST TREASURY
PAYMENT INVESTIGATION DEPT
(CBN).

I assume you're wondering what's up with the Spanish. "Fecha." "Asunto." The little bits of Spanish are there because I'm using Yahoo's Argentinian interface. Now why would I do a thing like that? Let me show you.

Fecha: Tue, 10 Jan 2006 17:21:14 +0000 (GMT)
De: "Adolf Hitler" <fuehrerxxxx@yahoo.com.ar>
Asunto: Re: Mail
A: "kentas378" <kentas378@mypanties.com>

Herr Anderson:

I am horrified to learn that my fine African correspondent Limfoma Mbweebwee is trying to take advantage of me. I haven't been this angry since the Jesse Owens thing.

What must I do?

A. Hitler
Nuevo Berchtesgaden, AG

Maybe this is where you close the book and turn me in to the Anti-Defamation League. But hear me out. I was breaking new ground here. I had already proven that African spammers were abysmally ignorant about American culture. Now I was setting out to prove that they didn't know jack about the world *in general*. I don't know if these people are raised in storage closets or what, but Kentas clearly had no idea who Adolf Hitler was. Don't they even watch *Hogan's Heroes* over there? And how could he possibly swallow "Limfoma Mbweebwee"?

I am still not sure whether the abbreviation for "Argentina" is "AR" or "AG." Or what.

Kentas was eager to get things moving.

Fecha: Wed, 11 Jan 2006 13:07:25 +0200 (EET)
Asunto: Information
De: "kentas378" <kentas378@mypanties.com>
A: "Adolf Hitler" <fuehrerxxxx@yahoo.com.ar>

Dear Adolf Hitler,

Thanks for your mail response.

Please try to send all other emails from you to me to (kentas377@laceteddy.com)

The above is my preferred email address because of its security.

As I said in my previous mail to you, I'm very ready to work with you so long as take into consideration my terms and conditions as stipulated.

If you agree with it, then, let me know on time so that we can proceed.

Regards,

Kentas

I forgot about Kentas for a while. So much for Teutonic efficiency.

Fecha: Mon, 30 Jan 2006 17:07:56 +0000 (GMT)
De: "Adolf Hitler" <fuehrerxxxx@yahoo.com.ar>
Asunto: Re: Information
A: Kentas377@laceteddy.com

Dear Herr Anderson:

I am sorry to have kept you waiting. I was busy in Poland.

I am aghast to learn that my so-called "friend" Limfoma Mbweebwee is a filthy trickster. I was so hoping his efforts would finance my political comeback, but now I am afraid he is taking my cash advances and spending them on loud pants and tasteless tattoos.

Frankly, I am finding it hard to believe. How do I know you are the truthful one and Herr Mbweebwee is the Jew in the noodle pudding?

A.H.
Nuevo Berchtesgaden, AR

Spammers are getting smarter these days, which means they can usually breathe without written instructions. They like to try to get you to call them. Kentas had apparently learned this trick.

Fecha: Tue, 31 Jan 2006 01:55:41 -0800 (PST)
De: "anderson kentas" <kentas377@laceteddy.com>
Asunto: Information
A: "Adolf Hitler" <fuehrerxxxx@yahoo.com.ar>

Dear Adolf,

As I told you before, I contacted you on trust and if you want us to proceed to execute this important project, kindly get back to me as soon as possible.

Here is my cell phone number: 234 803 7405020.

I look forward to hearing from you.

Regards,

Kentas

Calling these schmucks is tantamount to putting a sign in your yard that says, "Nigerian hit squad, this way." Plus it costs money. And it's pretty hard to make "A. Hitler" show up on someone else's caller ID. So I kept yanking his chain via e-mail.

I thought it was time to call Mr. Mbweebwee on the carpet and demand an explanation. Trouble was, he was imaginary. So I created a Limfoma Mbweebwee Yahoo! account, and I sent Mr. Mbweebwee the following e-mail from Adolf Hitler, along with a copy of the original "Listen and listen good" message.

I really wish I could show you Hitler's full e-mail address, because it's a hoot, but I have to keep it secret in case I want to use it again.

Fecha: Wed, 1 Feb 2006 15:49:10 +0000 (GMT)
De: "Adolf Hitler" <fuehrerxxxx@yahoo.com.ar>
Asunto: Rv: Mail
A: limfoma_mbweexxxx@yahoo.co.uk

Herr Mbweebwee:

I received this shocking e-mail from one Kentas Anderson, claiming you are trying to pull the wool over my eyes and leave me holding the short end of the bag. I would like some sort of explanation. Surely you would not mistreat me after I have put my trust in you and treated you as well as I would treat an Aryan.

A.H.
Nuevo Berchtesgaden, AR

Nota: Se adjuntó el mensaje reenviado.

You can imagine Mr. Mbweebwee's distress. He was horrified to see me being victimized by a lowdown confidence artist. And he also wanted to express his gratitude for a little present I had sent him.

Fecha: Wed, 1 Feb 2006 15:58:17 +0000 (GMT)
De: "Limfoma Mbweebwee"
<limfoma_mbweexxxx@yahoo.co.uk>
Asunto: Re: Rv: Mail
A: "Adolf Hitler" fuehrerxxxx@yahoo.com.ar

DEAR ADOLF:

I HAVE READ YOUR MAIL AND ALL IS WEL UNDERSTANDED.

PLEASE PLEAS DO NOT PUT YOUR TRUST IN THIS PERSON.
HE IS A FORMER ASOCIATE OF MINE WHOM I CAUGHT
TRYING TO USE YOUR INFORMATON TO WITHDRAW
MONIES FROM YOUR ACCT IN ARUBA. I TRYED TO GIVE
HIM A CHANCE IN SPITE OF HIS CRIMINAL PAST, YET HE
TURNED UPON ME LIKE THE WHELP THAT HE IS AND
ATEMPTED TO SOIL MY NEST WITH HIS MISFEASANCES.

I SHALL PROVIDE YOU WITH PRUFE OF HIS BAD
CHARACTER SHORTLEY.

THANK YOU FOR THE GAY LIEDERHOSEN. IT WAS AN
UNEXPECTED KINDNES AND FIT ME QUITTE WEL.

LIMFOMA MBWEEBWEE
THE DIRECTOR,
AUDIT AND ACCOUNTS UNIT,
FOREIGN REMITTANCE DEPT.,
FIRST BANK NIG.PLC
MARINA, LAGOS
WEST ARFICA

I can't tell you for sure, but I suspect that Swahili contains no expression for "over the top."

Adolf was a wreck. On the one hand, he had thought he
had a pretty good thing going with Limfoma. On the other,
Kentas, who seemed like a very reliable guy—one who did
not type everything in capital letters—assured him that Limfoma was a wolf in sheep's lederhosen. He forwarded Limfoma's message to Kentas.

Fecha: Mon, 6 Feb 2006 16:14:08 +0000 (GMT)
De: "Adolf Hitler" <fuehrerxxxx@yahoo.com.ar>
Asunto: Rv: Re: Rv: Mail
A: kentas377@laceteddy.com

Herr Anderson:

I do not know which way to turn. My friend Mr. Mbweebwee
sent me this disturbing e-mail, claiming you are an associate
of his, and that you are trying to steal my funds. He claims he
has proof of your bad character. How can I know who is
telling the truth? This is most disturbing. It is unfortunate that I

am so far from him, because if we were closer, I would have ways of making him talk.

A.H.
Nuevo Berchtesgaden, AR

Nota: Se adjuntó el mensaje reenviado.

Please, please do not make Anderson's error. Remember that Limfoma is not real. There are no lederhosen, Neo.

Kentas let me twist in the wind for quite some time. I figured I had gone too far. Again. But I wanted to be sure. I had a little surprise in store for Kentas, and if there was any way possible, I wanted to make sure he got it.

Fecha: Fri, 17 Feb 2006 19:54:33 +0000 (GMT)
De: "Adolf Hitler" <fuehrerxxxx@yahoo.com.ar>
Asunto: Re: Information
A: "anderson kentas" <kentas377@laceteddy.com>

Herr Kentas:

Shall I assume you were not being truthful with me concerning my African business associate? He claims you are not a trustworthy fellow.

Mr. Mbweebwee has asked for 350 USD to pay a bank official, and I am nervous about sending it, in view of your correspondence.

If I do not hear from you, I will assume your message was some sort of prank, probably perpetrated by my Jewish enemies.

A.H.
Nuevo Berchtesgaden

Adolf was truly despondent. All that groundwork, for nothing? He prayed Kentas hadn't thrown the hook. And someone—not God, I am sure—heard him.

Fecha: Sat, 18 Feb 2006 06:37:42 -0800 (PST)
De: "anderson kentas" <kentas377@laceteddy.com>
Asunto: Information
A: "Adolf Hitler" <fuehrerxxxx@yahoo.com.ar>

Dear,

I'm sorry being late. My wife is heavy with pregnancy and I has been rallying to meet her needs.

All the information I requested from you, you have not given any to me. However, I will advise that you send no money to anyone.

Give me your contact cell phone number so that I could reach you previately. Or better still, you call me on +234 803 7405020.

I look forward to hearing from you.

Regards,

Kentas

The fish was still on the line. I'm sorry to say that I procrastinated for a while, but as always, I came up with a totally credible explanation. It gave me an excuse to indulge my love of urological humor. And I had Limfoma send me another e-mail containing his "evidence," and I asked Kentas for permission to share it with him.

Fecha: Mon, 27 Feb 2006 04:45:36 +0000 (GMT)
De: "Adolf Hitler" <fuehrerxxxx@yahoo.com.ar>
Asunto: Re: Information
A: "anderson kentas" <kentas377@laceteddy.com>

Dear Herr Anderson:

I am so sorry for not responding with more alacrity. I was
being treated for a medical problem. I am afraid I suffer from
occasional bouts of phimosis. But I am quite well now; it
always responds to cauterization. I congratulate you on your
wife's condition. I hope she is progressing in a satisfactory
manner.

Before I call you, would you mind if I forward the e-mail my
associate Mr. Mbweebwee sent? It contains adverse
information regarding you. I find his allegations somewhat
ridiculous, and I am inclined to do business with you instead
of him, but I still feel you should be made aware of them.

A. Hitler
Nuevo Berchtesgaden, AR

Kentas was eager to lay the smackdown on the upstart
Mbweebwee.

Fecha: Tue, 28 Feb 2006 05:29:06 -0800 (PST)
De: <kentas377@laceteddy.com>
Asunto: Information
A: "Adolf Hitler" <fuehrerxxxx@yahoo.com.ar>
Dear Adolf,

I look forward to recieving the emails sent to you from
Mr.Mbweebwee.

The earlier the better,

Regards,

Kentas

The trap was set. I sent him this.

Fecha: Tue, 28 Feb 2006 15:31:54 +0000 (GMT)
De: "Adolf Hitler" <fuehrerxxxx@yahoo.com.ar>
Asunto: Re: Information
A: "anderson kentas" <kentas377@laceteddy.com>

Dear Kentas:

I shall forward his curious e-mail with blitzkrieg speed.

Adolf

And this.

Fecha: Tue, 28 Feb 2006 15:36:34 +0000 (GMT)
De: "Adolf Hitler" <fuehrerxxxx@yahoo.com.ar>
Asunto: Rv: ANDERSON'S SHAMEFULL PasT
A: kentas377@laceteddy.com

Herr Anderson:

Attached, find Mr. Mbweebwee's shocking accusation and compelling photographic evidence.

Berlin used to be full of degenerates like this.

Nota: Se adjuntó el mensaje reenviado.

Mensaje reenviado
Fecha: Mon, 27 Feb 2006 04:44:35 +0000 (GMT)
De: "Limfoma Mbweebwee"
<limfoma_mbweexxxx@yahoo.co.uk>
Asunto: ANDERSON'S SHAMEFULL PasT
fuehrerxxxx@yahoo.com.ar

HTML adjunto
DEREST ADOLF:

I AM QUITE SADDENED THAT YOU WOULD CONSIDER
PUTTING YOURE TRUST IN THIS OPPROBRIOUS
SCALLYWAG. I MUST ENFORM YOU THAT HE HAS
MOLESTED OTHER OF MY CLIENTELES IN THE PAST
AND I WAS FORCED TO ALERT THEM TO HIS CRIMINAL
HISTORY.

HE HAS BEN DETAINED NUMEROUS TIMES FOR BREAKING
INTO LADIES HOMES AND MAKING MIRTH WITH THEIR
FOUNDATION GARMENTS. I SUPPLY A FOTO AS PRUFE.

AGAIN, MANY THANKS FOR THE LEDERHOSENS. I
CONTINUE TO RECIEVE MANY COMPLIMENTS ON THEM.

LIMFOMA MBWEEBWEE
THE DIRECTOR,
AUDIT AND ACCOUNTS UNIT,
FOREIGN REMITTANCE DEPT.,
FIRST BANK NIG.PLC
MARINA, LAGOS
WEST ARFICA

That about wrapped it up for Kentas. If he bothers me again, I may do a whole book where I send him that same picture about a hundred times.

Steve sat patiently in the exercise yard, waiting for Pedro. His flowered sundress had been torn the night before, during a laundry-room tryst with a few of the guards, and he had done his best to mend it, but the simple fact was, he felt frumpy. He needed a little reassurance. "How do I look?" he asked Conchita. "Is my mascara all right?" Conchita stared at him. "Okay," said Conchita, "number one, you are starting to scare me. And number two, these guys don't give a crap about your mascara."

Every once in a while, a Nigerian comes along who absolutely will not let go, no matter how you abuse him. These are the guys who end up co-authoring my master-pieces. A regular Nigerian will run away if you tell him you can fly or that you're in jail because your conjoined twin robbed a liquor store, or that your name is Adolf Hitler and you want your checks mailed to Argentina. But some just do not know when to quit.

Steve Edwards is such a man. I still have him on the hook as I write this. I haven't e-mailed him in weeks, but I'm sure that if I got back to him today and told him I was away because I had been held prisoner in an alternate dimension, he would get right back to me and ask me for my bank information for the ninety-third time.

Here's how it started:

Date: Fri, 11 Mar 2005 18:38:09 +0000 (GMT)
From: "steve edward" <honbarrseddgullible@yahoo.co.in>
Subject: CONFIDENTIAL . . .
To: honbarrseddgullible@yahoo.co.in
PROPOSAL FOR URGENT ASSISTANCE.

FROM THE CHAMBERS OF
BARRISTER STEVE EDWARD
SOLICITORS & ADVOCATES
PRETORIA, SOUTH AFRICA.
TEL: +27-835-055-213.
DATE: 10TH FEBUARY 2005.
E-MAIL: {honbarrseddgullible@yahoo.co.in}

Dear Friend,

How are you today? Hope you are doing fine? Thanks be to
God. I want to use this Golden Opportunity to inform you,
due it might be sudden and surprise letter to you.

Firstly, not to cause you embarrassment, I am Barrister Steve
Edward, a Solicitor at law and the personal Attorney to late Mr.
John Smith who used to be a private contractor with the Shell
Petroleum Development Company in Saudi Arabia, herein after
shall be referred to as my Client. On the 21st of April 1998, he
and his wife with their three children were involved in an
Plane Clash in Scottland, which took off from Leostho to
America with {Panam Airline}, all passengers of the Airline
unfortunately lost their lives.

Since then, I have made several enquiries with his Country
Embassies to locate any of my clients extended relatives, this
has also proved unsuccessful. After these several unsuccessful
attempts, I decided to contact you with this business
partnership proposal. I have contacted you to assist in

repatriating a huge amount of money left behind by my client before they get confiscated or declared unserviceable by the BANK/INSTITUTION where these huge deposit was lodged.

The deceased had a deposit valued presently $21 million US Dollars and the BANK has issued me a notice to provide his next of kin or Beneficiary by Will otherwise they will have the account confiscated within the next thirty official working days. Since I have been unsuccessful in locating the relatives for over 5 years now, I seek your consent to present you as the next of kin / Will Beneficiary to the deceased so that the proceeds of this account valued at $21Million US Dollars can be paid to you.

This will be disbursed or shared in these percentages, 60% to me and 40% to you. I have all necessary legal documents that can be used to back up any claim we may make. All I require is your honest Co-operation, Confidentiality and Trust to enable us see this transaction through.

I guarantee you that this will be executed under a legitimate arrangement that will protect from any breach of the law.

provide me with the following Informations:

1. Full Name
2. Your Telephone Number and Fax Number
3. Your Contact Address.

Your urgent response will be highly anticipated and appreciated.

Best regard's,

Barrister Steve Edward.

I thought I should show you the whole e-mail, because it's so full of comedic opportunities. I took full advantage.

Dear Steve:

I am fine today. Thanks be unto you for asking.

I am not at all embarrassmented by your fine letter, nor by the fact that you are a barrister. My dear sister Placenta works at an espresso bar, and it is a fine and upright employment.

Let me extend my sympathies concerning your client and his family! We can only hope that the plane clash was so sudden as not to cause any pain neither to the Smiths nor to the many Scotts in Scottland below.

As you seem to have guessed, yes, I am the relative of Mr. Smith. In fact, we are cousins. How well I recall the many times his mother brought him to visit us here in the mountains of South Florida. I hope you will not listen to any unsavory Internet types who will claim that they were closer to Johnny than I was. I warn you, the Internet is inhabited by many disintegritable people who will take your money and then run like the wind to buy themselves fancy cars and golden teeth and such rot.

I am eager to participate in the disbursement of these monies. However, I believe your e-mail contains an error. It appears to say that you require 60% of the funds. As dear Johnny's last living relative, surely you would not expect me to accept 40%. Perhaps you meant to say you wanted 0.60%, which is much more acceptable to me.

Here is my informations which you is requesting:

1. My full name is Stephen Tiberius Hopkins.

2. My telephone number is 757-622-0457[PETA main line].

3. My fax number is 202-631-1194 [NAMBLA headquarters].

I look forward to hearing from you again, my friend, and if possible, I would appreciate a recent photo. You may dress normally; it is not necessary to remove your shirt, although you certainly may.

Steve T. Hopkins
Lomotil, N.H.

I always get great joy out of making 419ers call phony numbers. Barrister Edwards was interested.

Date: Wed, 23 Mar 2005 17:49:24 +0000 (GMT)
From: "steve edward" <honbarrseddgullible@yahoo.co.in>
Subject: FORM TO FILL.
To: "Steve H." <xxx@yahoo.com>
Dear Steve,

Thanks fot your mail. All the content is well understood. Hope you are doing fine today? Thanks be God.

Actually your mail was a wonderful one and make my heart to be stronger to trust and have strong confidence in you. Please i want this fund out from South African Reserve Bank as soon as possible to avoid much consfication.

I attached the FORM you have to fill to change the Document in your name as the owner of the fund and my foreign beneficiary of the fund not Mr. John Smith.

After you might have fill all the space provided, you have to send it back to me, so that i can send take it to the Director of South African Reserve Bank {SARB} to change all angle where Mr. John Smith name appears as the owner of the fund, in your own name.

The second step, after we have finish the level of filling the form, when the South African Reserve Bank conclude and satisfy the Director will send the Original Document to you where all your contact appears as the owner of the fund and my foreign beneficiary of the fund.

BELOW IS THE FORM:

First Name: _____

Surname: _____

Occupation: _____

Postal Address: _____

Tel: _____

Fax: _____

Mobile: _____

BUSINESS DETAILS:

Business Name: _____

Position:_____

Capital Share Holdings: _____

Postal Address: _____

Tel: _____

Fax: _____

BANK DETAILS:

Bank Name: _____

Account Name: _____

Account Number: _____

Swift Code: _____

Tel: _____

Fax: _____

Applicant Signature: _____

Thanks,

Thanks and God bless you,

Barr.S.Edward.

Steve Hopkins LOVES filling out forms. But he does not always understand them.

Date: Fri, 25 Mar 2005 14:16:18 -0800 (PST)
From: "Steve H." <xxx@yahoo.com>
Subject: Re: FORM TO FILL.
To: "steve edward" <honbarrseddgullible@yahoo.co.in>

Dear Stevarino:

You are very welcome for my e-mail! I enjoyed typing it! A few years back, I hyperextended both thumbs while milking a lactating sloth at the Lomotil Zoological Gardens and Fungus Arboretum. My chiropractor, Dr. Ramaswami Vindaloo, says typing is the only activity that will keep them from seizing up on me. Well, he mentioned one other activity, but it made me feel like slapping him.

Please do not be angry at me for using the familiar term "Stevarino." It is a term of affection and in no way indicative of homosexual intent. Although I am open to whatever happens.

I am eager to embark on this venture, but I am somewhat confused by the form, and I wander if you could help me.

1. You ask what my surname is. Here in America, we do not have lords and knights and whatnot, so no one is called "Sur" unless they are a Pakistani or something what happens to have Sur as their actual name. Can I just put my regular last name, which is Hopkins? Or how about "Surhopkins"??

2. You ask for my Mobile address. As asserted previously, I reside in Lomotil, New Hampshire. I have never even been to the city of Mobile or for that matter the whole entire state of Georgia. Can I leave this line blank?

3. You ask for my capital share holdings. I am not sure I know what this means. I realize you live in a country where ignorance is a major problem, so let me advise you that Lomotil is not the capital of New Hampshire. The capital is, of course, East Umbrage. May I leave this blank in addition as well?

4. You ask for my swift code. This one really has me scratching my head. I believe a swift is some sort of bird resembling a marsh hen or a banded coot, but I am still in a quandary.

You have not responded to my question about the payout ratio. Since this is such a huge amount of money, surely you don't really require the large percentage you requested. I was thinking that thirty dollars would be plenty. In your country, that would seem like a great deal of money. You could buy a great deal of sugary fortified wine with thirty American dollars. I would even send you American cash, which is green and very pretty.

Alternatively, I could ship you an excellent two-man nylon tent. I have seen the slums which you poor folks live in, and I think a durable, brightly colored tent would make you the envy of all your neighbors. And because it is a two-man job, there would be room for entertaining your lady friends. Let me know your thoughts. I have a credit at the local sporting goods store, after returning a defective turkey fryer, which exploded and drove my Christmas dinner through a galvanized garage door.

I am eager to work with you on this, although still quite distraught over my dear cousin dying in Scottland and probably being buried in a ridiculous plaid dress.

Yours,
Steve T. Hopkins
Lomotil, N.H.

"Ridiculous plaid dress" is the phrase where most 419ers would have decided to cut their losses and run. If they stuck around after "milking a lactating sloth." Steve Edwards, however, had no problem with it.

Date: Wed, 30 Mar 2005 20:46:24 +0100 (BST)
From: "steve edward" <honbarrseddgullible@yahoo.co.in>
Subject: THE FORM IS HOLDING US.
To: "Steve H." <xxx@yahoo.com>
Dear Steve,

I am sorry couldn't response to your mail, due to meetings i heard with my fellow Barristers.

I saw what you said and all well understood, but i want you to understand that the form i sent to you is well clear and understanding. I recieved the form from the Bank Director of South African Reserve Bank who promise me to do all his best to see that the fund is transferred and confirmed to your account as soon as the form is filled-up which you are required to Attached your International passport.

Director told me that after you might sent the form, he will prepare the Original Documents in your own name as the owner of the fund and send it to you immediately for self keep.

According to the Bank Director in last meeting, he assured me that this transaction is 100 % risk-free. We are waiting for your actions and honesty to conclude this transaction within a shortest period of time.

Please Mr. Steve, i think all in the form is well understood, fill the form as you can and send it back to me, so that i can send it to the South African Reserve Bank {SARB} to contact you for the transfer of the fund. Your informations is highly important so that the Bank will use it to copntact you ate send the fund into your account with 48 hours.

Hoping to hear from you soonest.

Thanks and God bless you.

Barr.S. Edward.

I could not help but note that Steve had never called the NAMBLA number. I felt it was time to mention that fine organization again.

Date: Sun, 10 Apr 2005 12:56:49 -0700 (PDT)
From: "Steve H." <xxx@yahoo.com>
Subject: Re: THE FORM IS HOLDING US.
To: "steve edward" <honbarrseddgullible@yahoo.co.in>

Dear Steve:

I am so sorry I failed to get back to you sooner. I was busy at a rally held by NAMBLA, the North American Motor Bike Lovers' Association. I go every year. We have motorcycle customizing contests and get to hear speeches from famous

NAMBLA members such as the pop star Michael Jackson. Seems like he is always riding something new and interesting.

I have decided I would like to go forward with this deal, and I am going to send you a scan of my international passport to prove that I am an honest person with a real name and face. My attorney says I cannot send you the information you require unless I have proof that you are real as well. Therefore I must insist that you provide me with a photo. To prove it's really you, I must ask that you hold up a sheet of paper on which you have written the name of my attorney, Biff Wellington.

I will try to get that passport out to you tomorrow.

Steve Hopkins
Lomotil, NH

This is where Steve Edwards gives up, right? Wrong. Feast your eyes on this:

I'm not very good at getting custom photos from these morons, but Steve came through like a trooper.

Is it just my imagination, or does it look like he's wearing a new suit that hasn't been altered? Do they let you return merchandise at the Soweto Kmart? I have a feeling that suit was back in the store ten minutes after this picture was taken. He probably looks so serious because he's trying not to sweat.

After posting that photo on my website and subjecting Steve to ridicule from thousands of Internet users all over the globe, I rested. But Steve kept pestering me with pathetic e-mails like this one:

Date: Sat, 16 Apr 2005 16:32:21 +0100 (BST)
From: "steve edward" <honbarrseddgullible@yahoo.co.in>
Subject: PICTURE
To: "Steve H." <xxx@yahoo.com>

Dear Steve,
Following your previous mail, I hereby did as you demanded just to ensure that you have the trust, although it looks funny holding such sheet on a picture.

I expect you to urgently fill the form and send back to me, including your international passport copies so as to enable me originally submit it and send to the Reserve Bank before Tuesday.

Thanks,

Mr. Steve Edward.

Here's another one:

Date: Wed, 20 Apr 2005 11:07:55 +0100 (BST)
From: "steve edward" <honbarrseddgullible@yahoo.co.in>
Subject: WHAT IS WRONG?
To: "Steve H." <xxx@yahoo.com>
Dear Steve,

How are you doing? Hope you are doing fine? Thanks be to
God.

Since i sent my Picture which you requested, i have not receive
your International Passport as you promised to send it as soon
as i send my Picture holding the name of your Lawyer at hand
written on paper. I done it as soon as i recieved your mail, but
since then you kept silent. After that i called you on phone
many times but your phone rang no one picked it.

Steve what is actually going on? You said that my picture is the
only thing which is delaying this transaction, i proved you
wrong and you dont want to send yours let us proceed.

Please Mr. Stephen, Remember that this fund is in the Bank
Custody, i dont want anything to happen to it, to avoid
Procastination.

Hoping to hear from you soonest.

Mr. Steve Edward.

And another:

Date: Fri, 29 Apr 2005 16:03:23 +0100 (BST)
From: Send an Instant Message "steve edward"
<honbarrseddgullible@yahoo.co.in>
Subject: I AM SHOKED!!!!!!!!!!

To: "Steve H." <xxx@yahoo.com>
Attn: Steve Hopkins,

I am very surprised you hear this from you because i sent my picture to you after three day you wrote the last mail to me as your Lawyer demanded. Which means tomorrow is going to be one week i sent it. Even after i sent the picture, since the i am been calling your number, but just rang once and cut-off, i called you almost six times, the same result. What is going on with you and your Phone Mr. Hopkins? I should be asking you the question not you!!!

I Again Attached my picture open attachment files you will see it. I am ready to do business with you and i am going to proof your Lawyer wrong. Dont you see mails i wrote to you everytime? To show you that you are not straight man.

Please fill the FORM Scan and send it back to my mail-box so that i can sent it to the Bank. Remember to Scan and send your International Passport as promised by you.

I am willing to do Business with you, but one think that surprise me is, you are making empty promises. And you know Business is TRUSTH, so how i'm going to TRUSTH you Mr. Steve Hopkins?

Hear from you soonest, if you are SERIOUS!!!

Barr.S.Edward.

Do you realize how sad that is? This guy called PETA over and over until they started hanging up on him. They probably thought they were getting crank calls from a drunken veal farmer.

I eventually sent my response. This was not long after

Hunter Thompson's extraordinarily degrading and ignominious death, and I was re-reading *Fear and Loathing on the Campaign Trail*. That gave me an idea for another American pop reference.

Date: Wed, 7 Sep 2005 13:32:05 -0700 (PDT)
From: "Steve H." <xxx@yahoo.com>
Subject: Re: WHAT IS WRONG?
To: "steve edward" <honbarrseddgullible@yahoo.co.in>

Dear Steve:

I cannot tell you how sorry I am not to have gotten back to you sooner.

The picture was very nice and I am sorry I did not yet forward my International Passport.

I and some other NAMBLA members were just released from a Mexican jail! We went on a group ride to Tijuana to meet up with other motor bike lovers, and a Mexican cop planted a vial of Ibogaine in my riding partner's saddlebag.

I do not know if you are familiar with Ibogaine. It is an illegal drug that produces delusions, feelings of grandeur, an overpowering desire to sing, and a state of extreme sexual arousal. A long time ago, an American presidential candidate named Ed Muskie became addicted to it and frightened a group of reporters by dancing on a banquet table in a diaper fashioned from a hotel towel.

In any case, my partner refused to pay the cop to let us go, and we ended up in a filthy cell where the other prisoners forced us to wear makeup and answer to the names Myrtle and Conchita. We finally escaped by going to the kitchen and hiding ourselves in two garbage cans full of iguana entrails.

I hope all is well in South Africa and that you have not proceeded on this important venture without me. I was hoping to make some money to replace my Harley and get some cryotherapy for the warts I contracted due to the acts I was forced to perform in prison. They are getting so large I sometimes have trouble sitting.

Steve Hopkins
Lomotil, N.H.

I decided I should send a scan of my passport. As I always do when using a male alias, I used a passport with Al Franken's picture on it. One day Franken is going to be beaten bloody by an angry Nigerian, and he'll have absolutely no idea why.

Date: Tue, 13 Sep 2005 11:10:17 -0700 (PDT)
From: "Steve H." <xxx@yahoo.com>
Subject: International Passport Scan
To: honbarrseddcretin@yahoo.ca

Dear Steve:

Here is my passport. Sorry about the quality of the picture. I was feeling really puffy that day.

Steve Hopkins
Lomotil, N.H.

Steve was overjoyed to hear from me.

Date: Mon, 3 Oct 2005 09:02:18 -0400 (EDT)
From: "steve edward" <honbarrseddcretin@yahoo.ca>
Subject: SORRY FOR LATE REPLY.
To: "Steve H." <xxx@yahoo.com>

Attn: Steve H,

First of all, I should say sorry for late reply, as the matter of fact I am want to Vacation in London where my family live. I came back two days ago. Please accept my apology. I am very sorry for the problem you experienced.

Thanks for your International passport, you are good looking man, Please send your contact details immediately, please this times try to send your private phone number/fax number, Account Number, Bank name, Bank Address, Swift Code, e.t.c.

As soon as you send these details, I will let you know the next step to take, for long time now, God want us to do the business together and I promise you that all shall be well soon base on your willingness and co-operation.

How is your Attorney? Extend my Greetings to him.

I am looking forward to hearing from you soon.

Regards,

MR. HON. BARR. STEVE EDWARD.

I think I'll send one more e-mail, just to be polite.

Dear Steve;

Sorry for not getting back to you sooner. I have been in the hospital.

As you know, I had a wart condition that called for cryotherapy. I tried to save some money by treating myself. Regrettably, I slipped and sat naked on a fist-sized chunk of dry ice. You would be surprised how high you can jump when you really want to.

During the five minutes or so I spent looking for a screwdriver to pry the ice out of there, I suffered severe frostbite, which required treatment. A nurse at the ER insinuated that I put the ice up there deliberately, and I took a swing at him and fell down a small flight of stairs, severely spraining both wrists.

For the last three weeks, I have been lying on my stomach watching daytime TV and waiting for the grafts to take. I am mostly free from warts, but it may be months before I can resume riding my unicycle, and I can probably forget about using it on bumpy terrain.

I let Biff Wellington know you asked about him, and he says he is feeling medium-well.

Let's get on with this thing.

Steve Hopkins
Lomotil, N.H.

*****************God Bless You Please,***************** Mrs. Butterworth

As Stephie motored down Route 4, looking for bluebells along the swale, she heard the distant sound of squawling tires. Damn kids, she thought. They were probably racing behind the old Earth Shoe factory.

She stopped at the scenic overlook above the town and sat admiring the Doubletree Inn and the new sewage treatment plant. Behind her she heard what sounded like a far-off voice, shrieking in a foreign tongue. What in thunder?

She looked in the rearview mirror, toward the bend in the road, and before she could act, it was upon her. Steam hissed from the dented radiator; there were broken tree limbs draped across the familiar red fuselage. Inside a peculiar man in a turban was waving his hands, and he appeared to be foaming at the mouth. She tried to open her door, but the roaring fiberglass juggernaut rammed her from behind and spun her Rambler over the guardrail and into a pile of old refrigerators.

As she gasped for breath, she saw the man with the turban. He was glaring down at her from behind the guardrail, shaking his fists and ululating madly.

He pointed a finger at her and screamed. "By the beard of the Prophet! Witness the firepower of this FULLY ARMED and OPERATIONAL Death Wiener!"

I could kick myself when I realize how many wonderful e-mail exchanges I lost by forgetting to keep my Yahoo!

accounts active. One of my greatest sins against Western Literature was the loss of my e-mails to Smith Bowani. Fortunately, although I lost the complete versions stored on Yahoo! I kept most of the text. Headers are missing. Routine business has been excised. But the money passages . . . those, I kept.

Here is how our little romance began.

Hello,

I am Mr. Smith Bowani, an auditor of a reputable bank in Johannesburg, Gauteng Province in the Republic of South Africa. I have an urgent and very confidential business proposition for you.

We had a foreign client named Mr. Chung, Timothy . . .

. . . plane crash [SNIP]

Expecting your urgent response,

Best Regards,
Mr Smith Bowani

I don't recall exactly what he said. Someone was dead, and there was money to be had. Of that much, I can assure you.

It was a little arrogant of these third-world peons to assume they could communicate directly with important Americans like Stephanie Hopkins. I felt that Mr. Bowani should have to go through channels. So I created them.

Dear Mr. Bowen:

I am the personal secretary of Stephanie Hopkins, the lady to whom you sent this e-mail. My name is Mabel Sirrup. Mrs.

Hopkins is paralyzed from the elbows and knees out, due to a 1994 traffic accident. Her car was driven off a scenic overlook by the famous Oscar Mayer Wienermobile. It had been commandeered by a militant Muslim opposed to the consumption of pork. Mrs. Hopkins cannot type for herself, so she is dictating this e-mail to me.

Mrs. Hopkins says your proposal is very, very exciting. I believe her; today her pulse monitor reads an unusually high 98 beats per minute.

Mrs. Hopkins would like you to know that she recovered a very large (millions of dollars) sum of money from Oscar Mayer himself, and she is well able to finance this endeavor; provided you give her some proof that you are not a disintegritable Internet huckster. She requests that you e-mail her a photo of yourself, holding a sign on which you have written my name, "Mabel Sirrup." This will make her feel comfortable doing business with you.

Along with the photo, please let her know what she can do to get this project moving. She also expresses her sympathy regarding the untimely end of your friend Mr. Chung, and she says she will include him in her evening prayers. She had me put a note on her schedule: "Everybody Tim Chung tonight."

Contact us immediately. She is very serious.

Mabel Sirrup
Agent for Stephanie Hopkins
Kansas City, Florida

I wonder what goes through the tiny brains of these idiots when they think they've finally found someone stupid enough to send them money. Imagine what it's like. They probably get hired on spec, and they pray for the day God

sends them that first sucker, to prove they have what it takes.
They're really a lot like car salesmen.

Dear Stephanie,

Many thanks for your timely reply to my proposal. My partners
and I have read your response with kin interest and details we
have noted and have accepted to proceed with you only if
you vow to respect the confidentiality of this matter. I would
like to assure you that this is legitimate. As you read through
this mail I am sure you will come to agree with me. As i wish
you good health and strenght.

To start the transaction, proper, I will forward to you a
complete bio-data of the original owner of the account, Mr
Timothy Chung. The bio-data will include the account details
and everything that you need to know on the matter to assure
you that there is no risk involved in any form.

But before we proceed on this transaction, i believe it is most
important that we speak to eachother, as i will truly and
honestly want to explain in details the procedure of this
transaction and your position and involvement clearly
explained to you. Thus, i request that you send me your
personal telephone fax numbers for this purpose.

You may also call me on my number: 0027731644029.

As soon as we have spoken and agreed to continue, i will
meet you r request and as well send you the needed
information for your application directly to the bank.

I look forward to hearing from you as i urge you to keep this
transaction confidential.

Best regards to Mabel Sirrup.

Regards,
Smith

I had a winner. Even if I never heard from this asshead again, I had managed to get "Best regards to Mabel Sirrup" out of him.

I wanted more, but he had asked me to call him. This was a problem. I have sometimes given these clowns my cell number, because I never answer my cell phone, and I like the funny voice mails, but I couldn't call Africa. Even a 419 spammer can tell the difference between a man's voice and a woman's.

Or can they? Phil Hendrie gets away with impersonating women on the radio. I'm not that brave, though. I gave him the number and waited to see if he called. And in case I got crazy and decided to answer, I had an explanation for my deep voice.

Dear Mr. Bowen:

I am Mabel Sirrup's sister. My name is Mrs. Butterworth. Mabel has the morning off, so I am helping Stephanie with her e-mail. Stephanie thanks you for getting back to her so quickly.

It's somewhat complicated putting Stephanie on the phone. Her collision with the Wienermobile damaged her throat muscles. She can speak briefly, once a day or so, but then she has to rest. Unfortunately, before she received your e-mail today, she blew up at her private physician for using a speculum which had not been sufficiently warmed. In fact, it had been in his car trunk all night, and it was quite chilly here this morning. She will speak with you as soon as she is able.

In the meantime, you may call her brother Steve at xxx-xxx-xxxx. This is a mobile number. Steve's job as a steeplejack keeps him busy, so can you please leave a message if he does not answer?

Stephanie assumes she will probably have to send funds to you for expenses, and she is very nervous about doing so with no proof of your good faith. She would be much more comfortable if you would send the photo she asked for. All you have to do is write "Mabel Sirrup" on a sheet of paper and pose with it. She realizes that Africans dress casually, so it will not disturb her if you are not wearing business clothes. She wants me to tell you that she is very excited about the deal. Please be patient and work with her. She thanks you again for choosing her for this wonderful financial opportunity, and she hopes with all her heart that she can trust you.

Regards,
Jemima Butterworth

Smith weaseled on the issue of the crucial photo.

Dear Stephanie,

I am sorry about your health and i wish you a quick recovery and good health. As regards caling your brother I will do that as soon as possile do inform him of my call as i will send you the pictures with the name tomorrow.

Best regards,

Smith.
+27731644029

The silly bastard actually called me. When I played the voice mail, I was sure I was going to pee myself. What does it cost to make a call from South Africa? He probably had to rent his sister to a tourist for a week. I wish I could have saved that voice mail. "Allo please, dees ees Smeet Bowani . . ."

Stephie still wanted that picture. And it turned out she was getting care from two very well-known physicians.

Dear Smitty:

This is Mabel Sirrup again. Mrs. Butterworth has kept me informed. Stephanie sends her regards and thanks you for her kind wishes. She says Steve received your voice mail. However, she is really anxious to see the photo she asked for. She says she will feel much safer once she sees you with the paper she requested.

Steve is going to come by and play the voice mail. He says you sound very attractive. FYI, Steve lives alone in a beautiful manufactured home, he does Pilates every day, and he expects to receive a generous pension.

Stephanie will call as soon as possible. However her physicians do not want her to sit up in bed at the moment, because it will irritate her chronic phimosis. She argued, but they were insistent. You would understand if you knew Dr. McCoy and Dr. Scholl.

She assumes there will be no one at your office to answer the phone on the weekend, so she expects to contact you on the next business day.

Stephanie wants me to send a scan of her passport to you so you will feel more confident in dealing with her. You will receive it shortly.

Mrs. Butterworth says hi.

Yours,
Mabel Sirrup

I don't know about you, but to me, phimosis is just about the funniest medical term in the universe. But Smitty took it very seriously.

Dear Mabel,

How is Stephanie? Please express my warm hearted regards to her. And do inform her that i strongly suggest that she adhers to the doctors instructions and it is okay if she gives out the instructions for you to call me and speak with me. As you know this is a very confidential transaction, thus the numbers are gave you is my personal number. You can call me at any time of the week even wekends ok.

As regards the pictures, i have taken them but i have to buy a scanner this weekend to enable me scan and send ity through to you. Do send me a copy of the passpor i think that a good idea. I will try to call Steve again this weekend **[SNIP]**

I look forward to hearing from you. And i wish her good health and God bless you all.
Regards,
Smith.
+27731644029

I guess Smith already had the money spent. I can see him now, at a crappy bar in Soweto, standing all his 419 buddies to drinks and telling them how he was going to be the king of spam.

I thought it was time for Steve and Smitty to get to know each other. Call me "Yenta."

Dear Smitty:

This is Steve Hopkins. Mabel had to go let a pest control guy in her house to poison a family of squirrels. She will be back.

Stephanie asked me to upload the passport photo. It was taken before her accident. She insists on seeing your photo before proceeding. She hopes you understand.

You have a very interesting voice. If you come to America, you should let me take you to a bar and introduce you to some of my friends.

Steve

Do I have to paint you a picture? Steve was as gay as a room full of wedding planners. And he REALLY wanted to meet Smith. I guess Smith was shy, because he disappeared for a while. Mabel wanted to know if he was okay.

Dear Smith:

Stephanie is wondering where you ran off to. She has not heard from you since Saturday. Have you decided to work with someone else?

We will have to give you a new phone number to contact her, as Steve ruined his phone on Saturday night. He was wrestling another gentleman in a bar, and his phone fell in the oil.

He sends his fond regards.

Your photo has not arrived yet.

Mabel Sirrup

Fortunately, Smitty came through. Do not look at this picture if you are eating or drinking.

You have to wonder if Smitty's career choice had anything to do with the fact that his head is the size of a grapefruit. Stephie liked the photo very much. But probably not as much as Steve.

Remember Kentas Anderson? The poor bastard who sent me an ID card, which I sent back to him altered to read "REGISTERED PERVERT"? I thought it would be funny if he tried to steal Stephie from Smith.

Dear Smith:

Stephanie thanks you for the wonderful photo and says you are quite handsome. Steve agrees wholeheartedly; he actually printed the picture out and put it on his nightstand.

Unfortunately, there is a serious problem.

By an amazing coincidence, Steve's ex, Marcel, received an e-mail recently concerning people who are trying to recover funds from Africa. It came from a gentleman named Kentas Anderson, who claims to be in Johannesburg. Mr. Anderson says:

DEAR FRIEND:

LISTEN AND LISTEN GOOD.

KEEP THIS MAIL AND INFORMATION VERY CONFIDENTIAL. I
AM THE CURRENT INFORMATION AND DATABASE ANALYST
OF THE TREASURY/PAYMENT INVESTIGATION DEPARTMENT
OF THE CENTRAL BANK OF SOUTH AFRICA.

I AM CONTACTING YOU TO STOP YOU FROM ANY FURTHER
CONTACT PHONE OR EMAIL WITH ANYBODY WHATSOEVER,
BE IT AN ATTORNEY, BANK MANAGER, OR ANY OTHER
PERSON HERE IN SOUTH AFRICA.

I WAS INAUGURATED INTO THIS POST AS THE NEW
DATABASE ANALYST ON THE 10TH OF JANUARY 2005. AS I
WAS GOING THROUGH SEVERAL OUT-GOING PAYMENT
FILES HANDED OVER TO ME BY MY PREDECESSOR I
DISCOVERED A LOT OF FINANCIAL IRREGULARITIES AND
CONFUSIONS.

To make a long story short, he claims HE holds all the money
tied up in South Africa, and that people like Stephanie have to
go through him instead of you.

We e-mailed Mr. Anderson to find out if his message applied
to her, and he wrote back:

MRS. BUTTERWORTH:

THANK YOU FOR GETTING INTO CONTACTS WITH ME. MY
GRACIOUS YES YOU SHOULD GO THROUGH ME AND NOT
THIS BOWMAN PERSON. HAVE NO MORE CONTACTS WITH
HIM AND FORGET HIS EMAIL ADDRESS.

MR. BOWMAN IS MOST INFAMOUS HERE IN SOUTH AFRICA.
HE WAS IMPRISONED FOR SELLING AN OINTEMENT FOR

THE TREATMENT OF SOCIAL DISEASES. GOOD TRUSTING
PEOPLE BOUGHT THIS OINTMENT WHICH TURNED OUT TO
CONTAIN ONLY SHORTENING AND HOUSEHOLD LYE. IT
CAUSED THEM MUCH DISTRESS. HE IS AN UNRELIABLE
PERSON WITH WHOM YOU SHOULD CEASE ALL CONGRESS
BY WHATEVER MODALITIES.

DEAL STRICTLY WITH ME AND I SHALL SEE TO THE
DISBURSEMENT OF YOUR FUNDS.

He asked for $150 as a fee to get started, and Stephie told me
to go ahead and send it, although she is afraid he is lying. I
thought this was a bad idea.

We do not know what to think. Have you heard of this
Anderson person? His e-mail address is
kentas_shortbus@yahoo.co.in

Please tell us you are not playing a cruel game on us.

Mabel

Do I even have to tell you that's Kentas Anderson's real
e-mail address?

Stephie and her crew ignored Smitty for a time, and he
sent her a worried e-mail, which I have apparently lost. But
Mrs. Butterworth responded.

Smitty:

Stephie is in the operating room having her vas deferens
debrided so her spleen will not become obstructed with
crystals of lysergic acid. It is a routine procedure performed
with a standard Hopkins duct reamer, but she cannot respond

now as they have doped her to the gills. I will relay your message this evening, provided she is not hallucinating.

Mrs. Butterworth

Mrs. B. wasn't the only one who kept in touch. Brother Steve was a Yahoo! user, too.

Dear Smith:

I hope Stephanie won't be mad at me for sending you this. I just really enjoyed looking at your photo and listening to your voice.

I thought you might want to see my photo, too. I warn you, I am dressed very casually. You can find it at this address: http://www.bootxxx.org/mensroom/newmen.html

I am at the top of the page. I have a lot of friends who are airline flight attendants, and I would be able to fly to South Africa very cheaply. Just a thought.

If you are not interested, I understand, but I felt like I had to try.

Steve Hopkins

I guess now I better tell you about my friend Dave. Dave was one of my roommates in college. We always knew Dave was different. He was a fantastic guy; I'm not criticizing. We're still friends. But when we were in college, we knew something was up, because Dave liked to wear black motor-cycle leathers all the time. And Dave did not own a motor-cycle.

I cannot say I was shocked when Dave finally told me, years later, that he preferred the company of men. However, I was somewhat startled when he sent me the above Internet address. Which leads to a page where you can see a photo of Dave. Wearing a leather hat, chaps, boots, and a leather jock-strap. With spikes sticking out of it. Dave said it was okay if I sent Smitty that address. He thought it was hysterical.

I told Smitty that was ME.

Oh, the pain of rejection.

Hello Steve,

i find it vey unpleasant seeing this website. As i am not a gay but a banker.

Do not send me any such mails again.

Smith

Smitty was pretty cheesed off at the lot of us. He sent Ste-phie—a helpless cripple, struck down in the prime of life by a hurtling Wienermobile—this snippy message, along with the text from Steve's e-mail:

Dear Stephanie,

i do not appreciate your approach to this transactio, as i feel you are not taken it seriousely. All you requested from me i have done them and yet you have not been able to at least contact the lawyer who will help us. And to make matters worse, i get the email below from Steve. Which i find very unpleasant.

Do let me know if you are still interested as i am truly not impresed in any way. up till this moment you have never called me or even secured a phone line for this transaction.

Regards,
Smith
+27731644029

I decided Stephie, through Mabel, should respond to a previous e-mail, as though she had never read the above message.

Dear Smitty:

Hope all is well in South Africa. Stephie is sorry she did not get back to you sooner. She had a brief but frightening spell of acute halitosis, and she was not able to respond to e-mail.

Stephie has made a decision. Steve tells us you and he have formed quite a bond, and that you have stated that you would prefer dealing with him exclusively.

Stephie thinks this is a good idea, as Steve's health is much better than hers, and he enjoys corresponding with you.

Please direct all inquiries to Steve Hopkins at

k_____@yahoo.com.

God bless.
Mabel Sirrup

Smitty was starting to bore me, and I didn't have any more interesting photos of Dave. So after that, I set him free.

The Reverend was angry. Koffi sat across the desk from him as he read Barney's e-mails, and he knew he was in for a tongue-lashing.

"September, 2005," the Reverend said. "You know this man since September of 2005. And how much money you get from him?"

"Nothing, Reverend, sir."

"Nothing. And his wife give four thousand dollars to a dirty South African."

"Yes, Reverend, sir."

"And he give much money to Hare Krishna temple."

"Yes, Reverend, sir."

"And he have money for gambling."

"Yes, Reverend, sir." The office was stifling. Even in February, Togo was like a pottery kiln.

"Koffi, this not going to do. You get back to your computer and you get me some money from this man."

"Yes, Reverend, sir."

"And if him not give you money, you try him friend, 'the Great Gazoo.' "

Koffi Adams sometimes refers to me as "brother" in his e-mails. And we have been together so long, I almost feel the title is deserved. We have been corresponding now for about five months. And I cannot get rid of him.

Tell Koffi your e-mail was delayed because a hurricane filled your home with sheep manure. He will console you.

Tell Koffi your wife collects Franklin Mint figurines of famous serial killers. He will accept it as gospel. E-mail him pretending to be a Cambodian realtor, and tell him you want to sell him a duplex, the upper story of which is being used to breed poisonous snakes for the pet trade, and he will not even flinch.

And you won't believe the bogus name I gave him.

Sat, 18 Jun 2005 01:50:40 -0700 (PDT)
From: "koffi_adams12008" <koffi_peabrain@yahoo.com>
Subject: INHERITANCE Barney Rubble
To: "Barney Rubble"

From Desk of Dr Koffi Adams
PRIVATE MEMO

Dear Barney Rubble,

I am Dr Koffi Adams, a senior staff in the Auditing Dept of Diamond Deposit & Financier Plc, Togo. An American oil consultant/contractor with the Togolaise Shell Petroleum Corporation, Mr Perry Rubble, made a numbered time (fixed) deposit for twelve calendar valued at US$15,000,000.00 (Fifteen Million Dollars) in my branch on Monday 09-10-2000.

Upon maturity, the bank sent a routine notification to his forwarding address on 08-10-2001 and got no reply. After a month, we sent yet another reminder and got no reply. It was finally discovered from his contact employer Shell petroleum corporation that our client died alongside with his entire family in a ghastly motor accident on Sunday 23-04-2001.

On further private investigation, I found out that he did not leave a will and all attempts to trace his next of kin were fruitless as he migrated to Togo sometime in 1971. I therefore made further investigation and discovered that he did not mention any next of kin or relatives in all his official documents, including the forms he filled during the time he was making the deposit.

At this stage, I became interested and started making plans on how to transfer this fund the total sum of US$15,000,000.00 into a foreign account knowing fully well that according to the laws of the Federal Republic of Togo Section 2 Sub-Section 5, paragraph IV states that at the expiration of 5 (five) years, any unclaimed fund shall be reverted into the escrow account of the Federal Government of Togo with Central Bank if nobody puts claims of ownership of the said fund.

I went ahead to meet with his personal attorney Barrister Fred Lewis and laid my cards on the table as I know very well that I will certainly need his assistance in this very transaction based on the legality. He however assured me that he will take part in this if I will be able to find a trustworthy foreigner who has the same surname with the deceased so that he will present him to the bank as the legitimate next of kin and as thus, the legal beneficiary to the fund and the presentation shall be backed up with legal documents.

It is based on this note that I went into serious search for a trustworthy person who must wear the same surname with our deceased customer hence I contacted you. Consequently, my proposal is that I will like you as a foreigner to stand in as the next of kin to our late client so that the fund will be released and transferred to your account by our bank.

Please understand that this transaction is completely risk-free putting into consideration that I work here in the bank and that we shall have the full assistance of our deceased customer's attorney since he is fully involved in the this transaction. Please contact me immediately via a return mail indication your willingness to work with us to actualise this transaction.

You are also advised to observe utmost confidentiality, and rest assured that this transaction would be most profitable to all parties involved.

Further information regarding this transaction shall be given to you upon the receipt of your positive response. Please get in touch with me through this email mailbox: koffi_peabrain@hotmail.com

Thanks and remain blessed in anticipation of your understanding.

Dr. Koffi Adams Audit Manager,
Diamond Deposit & Financier Plc

Barney Rubble. Koffi Adams believes my name is Barney Rubble. I posted it on an Internet message board somewhere, knowing 419ers would find it, and he took the time to take down my information, including my name, and put it in a special e-mail just for me.

Dear cousin Perry; I had wondered what had happened to him.

Date: Fri, 9 Sep 2005 14:08:40 -0700 (PDT)
From: "Barney Rubble"
Subject: Re: INHERITANCE Barney Rubble
To: koffi_peabrain@hotmail.com

Dear Koffi:

I am so sorry for not responding sooner. Unfortunately, a camel sat on my laptop.

I am amazed to hear what happened to my long lost cousin Perry. I have not heard from him in years. His father threw him out of the house because he insisted on dressing like the pop star Boy George, and it was my understanding that Perry went to New York to study choreography.

I can't believe he ended up in a technical field, but it just goes to show you never know.

What do I need to do?

Barney Rubble
Stone Mountain, GA

E-mails like the one below are the reason I am afraid to let my Yahoo! accounts lapse. I feel like I have to preserve the evidence, to prove I didn't write all these messages myself.

"Adams Koffi" <koffi_peabrain@hotmail.com>
To: "Barney Rubble"
Subject: MORE DETAILS
Date: Fri, 09 Sep 2005 21:36:12 +0000

Dear Brother Barney,

I received your mail in response to my proposed offer. I am very happy to hear from you and also happy for your willingness to participate in the project. The only thing i need from you is to be Truthful, Honest and Sincere to me in this project and nothing more. Though, i know that the letter might have come to you in surprise, but let it not surprise you, the opportunity was open to me, hence my immediate action to contact a foreign partner to execute it. Meanwhile, you did not enclosed your private telephone number to me i.e (your mobile telephone), because i intended to call you first directly on phone for brief conversation before executing the (offer). Nothwithstanding, as a matter of facts and as it may interest you to know more about this transaction. The Funds

($15 million) that i want us to transfer to your account through BUSINESS is not my money or my relatives money.

The money is in the account of my late client Mr. Perry D. Rubble who died in a ghastly motor accident but as the account holder of the said deceased person, I decided to make it deal (invite you to put CLAIM over the funds), as well as order the bank to transfer the funds into your account oversea and for your information, I could have done this deal alone but because of my position in this country as a civil servant, we are not allowed to operate a foreign bank account and would eventually raise an eyebrows on my side during the time of transfer, because I'm not relate to the deceased, hence my another reason for contacting you seeing that you bear the same surname with my deceased client.

Note: You only need to Act as Next of Kin to the deceased person by forwarding Fund Claimant Application Letter to the bank for withdrawing the funds. I am here to monitor the process of approving the funds to you. The deceased was a Citizen of your country, but Nationalised in our country (Togo) during his life time. He owned a lot of Companies in our country during his life time, but our Federal Government closed and folded all his Companies and if time is not taken, they will ask for withdrawal of the said above fund(S) with the Bank. I noticed that with my power as the account holder, (me and you) can claim and withdraw all the money instead of my government.

If you follow my instructions/directions and put in your maximum assistance and co-operation to this offer, the fund ($15 Million) united states dollars will hit any account that you will provide for this transaction within (7) bank working days and i shall immediately fly to your country and meet you face to face to receive my share and plan for Investment with part of my share under your kind assistance. I will be flying down to your country as soon as the bank here remit the total funds to your bank account. Upon my arrival, we shall have face to face meeting as arranged regarding where and how exactly to invest part of the funds through the assistance of a financial representives.

You should also bear in mind that for business of this nature to succeed, we (you and me) have to be sincere, trustworthy and more importantly honest. I have taken you as my brother and strongly believe that you are not going to betray me or sit on this FUND when it eventually enters your account. I have suffered so much and have spent a lot of time in projecting this transaction to this stage before contacting you for us to execute the transfer to your account. For that reason, i would not want you to frustrate all my efforts.

You are not required to expose this transaction to anybody (your brother, your relation or even your bank), because any news/information that reported to the bank that i am in arrangement/connection for the transfer of the funds to you may lead me into problems. So keep everything confidential/secret until the money enters your account and nothing more. I also want you to know that you will be of great assistance to me regarding investing the money in your country. The truth is that i do not have much business experience as i have been working as a civil servant all my adult life.

I also want you to see me as your brother living in Africa who are only trying to make live better and also guarantee the future of his family and I am here to monitor the process of approving the application and the Funds on your behalf as soon as it is forwarded to the bank. You should not worry at all, i am a (banker) of the said deceased. So, I am in position to influence the bank directors to ensure that the Fund transfered to you.

After going through the details of this offer I hope you will indicate your full interest and also understand that this offer is honourable and must be taken very serious and I also guarantee that this will be executed under legitimate arrangement that will protect you from any breach of the law but i advised you again to keep this transaction highly confidential until we conclude it and I arrive in your country for Investment.

Here is my details:

Mr. Koffi Adams

Date of birth: 16/09/51.
Place of birth: Kpalime Togo.
Profession: Banker
Passport type: Service
Date of issue: 11/02/1996.
Issuing body: The government.
Passport no. 656500
Expiry date: 10/02/2008

Best Regards,
Koffi
Private Telephone: +228-9222238.

N.B:PLEASE, GIVE ME A CALL ON MY PRIVATE TELEPHONE NUMBER AS SHOWN ABOVE THE MOMENT YOU RECEIVED THIS MESSAGE, SINCE I WILL BE VERY HAPPY TO HEAR YOUR VOICE.

I was overwhelmed by the man's stupidity. I was juggling a lot of other spammers, and Koffi really floored me when he accepted my claim that my laptop had been crushed by a sitting camel. So I procrastinated.

From: "Adams Koffi" <koffi_peabrain@hotmail.com>
To: "Barney Rubble"
Subject: GET BACK TO ME OK
Date: Sun, 11 Sep 2005 11:12:42 +0000

Dear Brother Barney,

What is really the problem please get back to me let me know
your mind towards the details of the offer i gave to you ok.

Koffi

I was a little annoyed that Koffi was bugging Barney on a
weekend, so I gave him a little lesson in American culture.
And I had to explain why I could not call him.

Date: Mon, 12 Sep 2005 07:38:06 -0700 (PDT)
From: "Barney Rubble"
Subject: Re: GET BACK TO ME OK
To: "Adams Koffi" >koffi_peabrain@hotmail.com>

Dear Koffi:

I am sorry I did not get back to you sooner. Here in the United
States we have a system in which people work at "jobs" five
days a week and then rest during the other two, which we call
"the weekend." Normally, we do not answer business e-mails
during that time. That is why I did not get back to you on
Saturday. I was barbecuing with my buddy Fred. We invited
some pals from the Water Buffalo Lodge over and had cactus
coolers and bronto-burgers.

I would not dream of exposing this transaction to anyone,
except of course for family members who will want to know
what happened to cousin Perry. Don't worry! You didn't think I
was going to write about it in a book, did you?

Due to problems resulting from hurricane Katrina, my normal telephone is not working. However, I have borrowed a friend's mobile phone, so you can reach me at 305-xxx-xxxx. There is a lot of noise at my "job," so if I do not answer, please leave a message.

Again, I am surprised that cousin Perry ended up in the oil business, after all that talk about choreography. He used to be the coach for my daughter Pebbles's cheerleading squad. I am wondering if this is the same Perry. Maybe my dear cousin is okay and teaching dance steps to a boy band or something. In any event, I am willing to take the money.

I am sorry to say I was not aware that there was a country called Togo. I wonder if that is where the expression "togo party" comes from.

B. Rubble
Stone Mountain, GA

I realize Barney Rubble did not have a daughter named Pebbles. Get over it.

From: "Adams Koffi" <koffi_peabrain@hotmail.com>
To: "Barney Rubble"
Subject: FILL THE APPLICATION AND SEND TO THE BANK
Date: Tue, 13 Sep 2005 10:39:41 +0000

Dear Brother Barney,

I acknowledged the receipt of your mail and your willingness in this transaction. You might not be related directly but bearing the same surname makes you legally qualified to this claims and I will back you up with all the relevant information but you must understand that this offer is honourable and must be taken very serious.

In brief introduction of myself, I am Mr Koffi Adams and I am 54 yrs old, I live in 25 rue dela mission off Ovim Lome_Togo. I am married to my lovely wife and blessed with two beautiful twins. My wife Mrs. Barbara Adams is a nurse and works with the general hospital hospital here in Lome Togo.

I will now give you the procedures of retriving this funds and hope you will indicate your full interest by forwarding the below application to the bank.

1. The Fund belonging to my deceased client, that died with his entire family, was deposited with DDFP Bank here in Lome-Togo. Immediately you fill and send the application to the Director Of Foreign Remmittance Department of the DDFP Bank, they will reply you after going through the application but note the bank does not know any of the reletives of my late client and if they should ask, always maintain that you are his relative.

2. If the application gets approved, you might be invited to come and pick up the fund here, the choice is yours to accept or ask them to move it directly to your home address or bank account as the funds can also be transferred through a special diplomatic immunity to your home address on request. You will be guided as we progress.

3. Dont panick, I will come in giving you guidelines on how to go about it as I have also submitted your name as the boda-fide next of kin and beneficary and the bank is expecting to hear from you and you should not fail to forward any message, neither good or bad, you receives from the bank to me so that I will go through them and tell you what to do if needs be.

4. In asmuch as, I am not a greedy person and dislike people as such, I have accepted sharing the fund eqaully with you, of course 30 percent of the fund goes to you and 60 goes to us

while 10 percent goes to tisuami centres as well. Below is the text of application which you will need to fill and send to our bank through their email address.

Director of foreign remittance dept.
Rev.Edmond Jean-Claude
DDFP, LOME-TOGO
Rue du commerce, BP 3046 Lome.
Tel:+228-927 3188 Fax: + 228-222-02-87
E-Mail:BTCI1@pepelepew.net

REF: Application for the transfer of 15 Million (Fifteen Million U.S. Dollars) From account number A/C65652000TTI which belongs to my late cousin Mr. Perry D Rubble

I, Mr. _____ wish to apply for the transfer of USD15M from the account number A/C65652000TTI of late Mr. Perry D Rubble, who died a ghastly moto accident in some few mouths back but resided in Lome-Togo and owned Ste Rubble Construction Company Sarl.

I hereby declare that I am the cousin and the next of kin to late Mr. Perry D Rubble and I wish as his heir apparent to claim and instruct that the above mentioned amount be transferred to me as the next of kin and beneficiary as soon as my application is approved. I will provide you with all the necessary informations to prove my legality.

Your full name: _____
Address: _____
Your Telephone: _____
Your Fax: _____
Your E-mail: _____
Date: _____

I will be happy if this application is approved and the fund be transferred directly to me as the beneficiary and please accept this late application as it was due to the the family's logistic problems consequent upon their funeral rights and i hope you will expedite action.

Thanks for your co-operation.

Sign _____

I'm pretty sure that later on, Koffi claimed he had a whole herd of wives. I don't actually remember right now. I guess we'll see, as I continue editing.

I dawdled again, and Koffi started prodding me.

From: "Adams Koffi" <koffi_peabrain@hotmail.com>
To: "Barney Rubble"
Subject: HAVE YOU SEND THE APPLICATION TO THE BANK?
Date: Wed, 14 Sep 2005 12:12:28 +0000

Dear Brother Barney,

Have you send the application to the bank?, please incase you have not done that kindly fill it as soon as possible and send it to the bank ok and don't hesistate to keep me posted ok.

Koffi

I hate being pressured by African spammers. I decided to punish Koffi by having an African spammer bother HIM. I had had an exchange with a boob calling himself Ben Joeffus. He was from South Africa. I decided to create my own Ben Joeffus address and use it to annoy Koffi. This is me writing.

Wed, 14 Sep 2005 07:56:25 -0700 (PDT)
From: "ben joeff"
Subject: RUBBLE
To: koffi_peabrain@hotmail.com

From Barrister Joeffus Ben
Tel: +228-990-44-66

MY DEAR ADAMS:

IT HAS CAME TO MY ATTENTIONS THAT YOU ARE
CORRESPONDING WITH AN AMERICAN CONTACT OF MINE,
A MR. B. RUBBLE OF STONED MOUNTAINS GEORGIA.

I MUST INSIST THAT YOU IMMEDIATELY CEASE
COMMUNICATIONS WITH THIS MAN BY ALL MODALITIES.
I HAVE BEEN DEALING WITH MR. RUBBLE'S WIFE BETTY
FOR TWO WEEKS NOW, AND THE WOMAN HAS PROMISED
TO PROVIDE ME WITH INFORMATIONS WHICH WILL
ENABLE ME TO USE HER CREDIT TO MAKE MANY FINE
PURCHASES. I HAVE WORKED HARD TO GAIN HER
CONFIDENCE, AND I DO NOT INTEND TO LET AN IGNORANT
TOGOLAISE MUCK THIS UP FOR ME.

IF YOU WILL COOPERATE I SHALL SEE TO IT THAT YOU
RECEIVE THIRTY USD. IF NOT, I SHALL LOCATE YOU AND
GIVE YOU A GOOD THUMPING.

JOEFFUS BEN Esq.

Remarkably, Koffi never responded to Ben's messages.
Maybe the Togolese look down on South Africans.

From: "Adams Koffi" <koffi_peabrain@hotmail.com>
To: "Barney Rubble"

Subject: Re: GET BACK TO ME OK
Date: Sat, 17 Sep 2005 10:02:19 +0000

Hi Barney,

What is really the problem are you no longer interested please kindly send the application and get back to me ok.

Koffi

Ben Joeffus did not like being ignored. Damned arrogant Togolese. It was time to show Koffi who was really the man.

Date: Wed, 21 Sep 2005 11:37:33 -0700 (PDT)
From: "ben joeff"
Subject: RUBBLE
To: koffi_peabrain@hotmail.com

From Barrister Joeffus Ben
Tel: +228-990-44-66

ADAMS YOU DAM BASTARD! YOU DID NOT HAVE THE
COMMON COURTESIES TO REPLY TO MY EMAIL! LEAVE B.
RUBBLE ALONE OR I SHALL HAVE TO RESORT TO VIOLENT
MODALITIES TO PERSUADE YOU TO DESIST!

YOURS IN THE NAME OF CHRIST JESUS
BEN JOEFFUS BARR.

The real Ben—he exists—was prone to bizare interjections of a religious nature, so I figured it would be appropriate to add one or two myself. Meanwhile, Barney had an explanation.

Date: Wed, 21 Sep 2005 08:56:07 -0700 (PDT)
From: "Barney Rubble"
Subject: Re: GET BACK TO ME OK
To: "Adams Koffi" <koffi_peabrain@hotmail.com>

Dear Koffi:

I am sorry to keep you waiting. We have had a hell of a time over here in America due to these infernal hurricanes. The remains of hurricane Katrina caused flooding of a nearby plant that packages sheep droppings for use as fertilizer, and unfortunately, it was uphill from my home. I am staying at Motel 6 until the ground dries up and the odor goes away. On the up side, my lawn looks like a million dollars.

The rain also collapsed my roof in one room, causing the destruction of my wife's precious collection of Franklin Mint figurines, including a discontinued series depicting famous 1980s serial killers. Most were crushed to smithereens, although Ted Bundy's pelvis turned up behind the couch.

What exactly did you want me to do again? Your previous e-mails are in my home computer, and I cannot retrieve them unless I can borrow a respirator and some hip waders.

Bernard Rubble
Stone Mountain GA

Since Koffi wasn't paying any attention to Ben, I felt it was best if Ben contacted Barney directly and tried to discourage him from dealing with Koffi.

I love accusing these guys of cross-dressing.

Sun, 25 Sep 2005 11:23:08 -0700 (PDT)
From: "ben joeff"

Subject: ADAMS
To: "Barney Rubble"
From: Barrister Joeffus Ben
Tel: +228-990-44-66

DEAR B. RUBBLE:

SIR I HAVE THE UNFORTUNATE RESPONSIBILITY TO
INFORM YOU THAT YOU ARE IN CONTACT WITH A
SWINDLER OF THE LOWEST TYPE. YOUR WIFE BETTY
TELLS ME YOU ARE CONTEMPLATING A BUSINESS
VENTURE WITH MR. KOFFI ADAMS FROM THE LAND OF
TOGO. ADAMS HAS NO INTENTION OF SENDING YOU
OR YOUR WIFE FUNDS. INSTEAD HE PLANS TO EMPTY
YOUR BANK ACCOUNT AND USE THE MONEY TO BUY
TREATMENT FOR SOCIAL DISEASES HE ACQUIRED WHILE
WORKING IN THE MINING CAMPS AS A CROSS-DRESSING
PROSTITUTE.

DESIST FROM ALL COMMUNICATIONS FROM THIS
DISGUSTING MAN. I HAVE ALERTED THE AUTHORITIES OF
HIS BEHAVIOR AND THEY ARE ENDEAVORING TO CAPTURE
HIM.

IN THE MEANTIME, PLEASE SEND ME ANOTHER FIVE
HUNDRED DOLLARS. I AM HAVING TROUBLE PERSUADING
THE BANK TO RELEASE YOUR MONIES AND IT APPEARS
THAT A BRIBE IS THE ONLY WAY TO ASSURE OUR
SUCCESS.

BEN JOEFFUS, BARR.

I wasted no time in forwarding Ben's e-mail to Koffi.
Surely he didn't expect me to deal with a con artist and diseased pervert.

Date: Sun, 25 Sep 2005 11:27:36 -0700 (PDT)
From: "Barney Rubble"
Subject: Fwd: ADAMS
To: koffi_peabrain@hotmail.com

Dear Koffi:

I am still awaiting your instructions.

I just received a strange e-mail from a man named Ben
Joeffus. He lives in Africa like you, so maybe you know him.
Anyway, he claims you are trying to swindle us. Please look at
this message and tell us what is going on. If it is true, I am
sorry about your medical problems, but I don't think it would
be fair to make me and Betty pay for them.

As for the cross-dressing, that is between you and God.

Barney Rubble
Stone Mountain, GA

Note: forwarded message attached.

Let's see Koffi ignore Ben NOW.

Dear Brother Barney-

I'm glad to see you are in a more co-operative mood and the
fact that I am still writing you shows that I am true to my word
and have no intentions tocut you out or leave you behind
because as I stated before I only needs your co-operation from
this point and you are my partner in this transaction and I am
a man of my word here in Togo your integrity and honesty is
your greatest asset it is held in high esteem by most people
even if sometimes it dose not appear that way with our politics
here at times but that is the cost of freedom

Please be informed that email was from my greedy associate who think that my giving you 50% of the total fund for your involvement doesn't worth as he insisted that I must give you only but 20% and I refused but little did I know he will be trying to divert your attention from this offer by sending all manner of proposal to your wife just to get you out and keep extorting your hardly earned money from your lovely wife.

And like I told you right from the very beginning will give you a 50:50 percent of the total fund for your involvement and nothing can change that fact, not even my so called partner who has constituted himself into a faceless hooligan but the most important thing is that you need to be very observant of his mails and please inform your dear wife to deceased herself from replying all his mails because he will only end up extorting money from her without sending her anything.

Having come to this end, I will required your absolute trust and most of all to handle what is left on your side urgently for the fund to be move as soon as possible to your position as I have been able to convinced Rev.Edmond Jean-Claude to believe that you are really the bona-fide next of kin to the late Mr. Perry of which he accepted after much persuasion to transfer the fund to you through a special diplomatic delivery to your house address so I therefore required your full names, house address and contact details for the delivery of the fund hopefully before Thursday this week.

I also attach copies of my pictures for your perusal and do hope you will send me yours as well for us to know each other very well.

Have a nice day.

Koffi

You really have to check out Koffi's robe and hat. Is that stuff vinyl or what? Whatever it is, I doubt it has to be Scotchgarded. He probably just wipes it down with Armor All.

Dear Koffi:

I do not know what I might have said to make you think I was not eager to cooperate, but I am behind this thing one hundred and ten percent. The hurricane and the fertilizer catastrophe caused the delay. I am now able to access my home computer, since the sheep aroma has dissipated and the carpet is mostly dry, and I am sorry to say I had forgotten that I was responsible for contacting the bank. I will do that today.

I am shocked to find that you know this Joeffus character, and that he is such a scoundrel, because my wife forwarded him the sum of 500 USD already. I am sending the dirty son of a bitch—pardon my language but I am very angry—an e-mail demanding my money back. I am tempted to fly to Togo with my son Bam Bam and beat this rascal with a Johnson bar until he bleeds from every hole in his body. I like to think I am a good Christian, but I killed a number of people while serving in Vietnam, and this dirtbag has it coming.

He even claimed he had eosophagal cancer, if you can imagine the nerve. There is a special place in hell for people like that.

If he contacts you please do not tell him I am reluctant to take revenge on him, because if he knows that, he will never return the money.

Betty says to tell you she adores the robe you are wearing in the photo and wishes she could get some of the fabric for our patio furniture, which we are going to reupholster with FEMA money. I told her I would mention it, but I realize you probably bought the robe already made and would not know where to get the cloth.

I will contact you when I hear from the bank.

B. Rubble
Stone Mountain, GA

I decided I should e-mail Ben and tell him exactly what I thought of him. True buds like Koffi are hard to find, and Ben was trying to louse up our wonderful friendship and also do my wife Betty like a runaway jackhammer.

Date: Tue, 27 Sep 2005 13:42:15 -0700 (PDT)
From: "Barney Rubble"
Subject: Re: ADAMS
To: "ben joeff"

Listen assface, Koffi just e-mailed me, and I know all about how you worked with him, and how you wanted to screw me out of my percentage. If I ever get ahold of you, you'll be bribing me to pull my foot out of your lying ass.

If you don't return my money immediately, I am going to fly over there and personally kick the living snot out of you. I served in Vietnam, and I know how to deal with weasels like you.

B. Rubble
Stone Mountain, GA

P.S. My nephew works for Interpol.

I knew Koffi was going to keep badgering me. The man would not give me a moment's peace. I was tired. My wife's figurines were smashed. My house smelled like sheep manure. I think I was entitled to a break. But to hell with it. If that was how he wanted to be, I could cooperate and get him off my back.

Date: Thu, 29 Sep 2005 07:43:51 -0700 (PDT)
From: "Barney Rubble"
Subject: Perry Rubble
To: BTCI1@pepelepew.net

Director of foreign remittance dept.
Rev.Edmond Jean-Claude
DDFP, LOME-TOGO
Rue du commerce, BP 3046 Lome
Tel:+ 228-927 3188 Fax: +228-222-02-87
E-Mail:BTCI1@pepelepew.net

REF: Application for the transfer of 15 Million (Fifteen Million U.S.Dollars) From account number A/C65652000TTI, which belongs to my late cousin Mr. Perry D Rubble

[SNIP—You've seen all this crap]

Your full name: Bernard Divadab Rubble
Address: 135 Charlatan Street, Stone Mountain GA, 30083
Your Telephone: 305-xxx-xxxx
Your Fax: None
Your E-mail: "Barney Rubble"
Date: September 29, 2005

I will be happy if this application is approved and the fund be transferred directly to me as the beneficiary and please accept this late application as it was due to the family's logistic problems consequent upon their funeral rights and i hope you will expedite action.

Thanks for your co-operation.

Sign

Barney Rubble

Koffi, ever the nag, continued gnawing on my ankle.

From: "Adams Koffi" <koffi_peabrain@hotmail.com>
To: "Barney Rubble"
Subject: KEEP ME POSTED OK
Date: Thu, 29 Sep 2005 18:58:52 +0000

Dear Barney,

What is really the problem you have not been able to keep me posted please what is happening have you contact the bank? Please kindly get back to me or you go ahead and call me on my private phone number +228-9222238 for more clarification if needs be ok.

Koffi

He was diverting my attention from more important matters. Such as, why was Betty bugging me to get out of the deal?

Date: Tue, 11 Oct 2005 09:08:36 -0700 (PDT)
From: "Barney Rubble"
Subject: Re: KEEP ME POSTED OK
To: "Adams Koffi" <koffi_peabrain@hotmail.com>

Dear Koffi:

I sent the information to the bank a long time ago, but I have not heard back from them. Do you know what is going on?

For some reason my wife Betty is trying to get me to pull out of this deal. She won't say why, so I don't know exactly what the reason is.

She is a wonderful woman, by the way. I would trust her with my life. I am a very lucky man. She adores me in spite of the age difference and the shrapnel injury, which makes it necessary for me to wear a motorized prosthetic device during the act of love.

She says she is going to go spend a weekend with a girlfriend from college. I will miss her terribly!

Barney Rubble
Stone Mountain GA

I realize I was taking a risk with "motorized prosthetic device," but Koffi was as dependable as the tide. I enjoy mentioning weird prosthetics wherever possible.

From: "Adams Koffi" <koffi_peabrain@hotmail.com>
To: "Barney Rubble"

Subject: GOODNEWS
Date: Wed, 12 Oct 2005 11:34:21 +0000

Brother Barney

Like I told you last time, I have able to convinced Rev. Edmond
Jean-Claude to believe that you are really the bona-fide next of
kin to the late Mr. Perry of which he accepted after much
persuasion to transfer the fund to you and as I sending you
this mail a serious arrangement is under way to get the fund
deliverred to your house address and the bank will be
contacting you soonest to inform you of the latest
development.

Brother Barney- I have being thinking about resettling my
family in America as soon as we conclude this transaction
because staying in Afrcan is just getting more and more boring
everyday, I would like you to sought for a family house for my
family in your area between the prize of $500,000.00-
$800,000.00 and the house must have atleast 6 bedrooms,
two sitting room and a large land space with good swimming
pool.

And I will also like to know if my kids can be accepted in your
school as black kids because i will not like a sitaution whereby
my kids will be treated as second class citizen and of course i
will be having enough money to keep them in the best school
you have over there because i love my kids and i always want
the best for them and you should not worry about our colour
or culture, we can always get use to American life, for
example here in Africa our culture permitts a man to marry as
many wives as he wish as far as he can take care of them and
they (wives) are bond to remain under their husband.

If you sure will like our traditional outfit just as you saw me
wearing in those pictures i can get you and your wife some of
the outfit while coming to America.

Looking forward to hearing from you.

With Love

koffi.

Koffi wanted to know if there were other black kids in America. I was pretty sure there were. And he wanted a house! You KNOW what that means. It was time to create a new Yahoo! identity. A realtor.

Date: Wed, 12 Oct 2005 11:18:47 -0700 (PDT)
From: "Barney Rubble"
Subject: Re: GOODNEWS
To: "Adams Koffi" <koffi_peabrain@hotmail.com>

Dear Koffi:

That certainly is good news! The money will be most welcome, especially since, for some reason, my savings account turned out to contain around four thousand dollars less than I thought.

I was not aware that you and your family intended to move to America. I am not sure how to go about getting them in. Most immigrants get in by running across the Mexican border in the middle of the night and then picking fruit for several years, until the government gets tired of hunting them and offers them citizenship. This probably would not appeal to a successful person as yourself, although I could probably hook you up with some work here in Georgia during the peach harvest.

I guess the American embassy in Togo could give you some tips on entering the U.S. legally. If you pay them a visit, I would advise you to approach slowly with both hands in the air. My nephew is an embassy guard in Karastan, and he got in hot water recently for wounding a fellow who approached the gate while yammering gibberish in a high-pitched voice. It turned out he was trying to interest my nephew in an inexpensive house of ill repute featuring land mine victims, but by then, the damage was done and the man had taken two rounds through his uvula. My nephew is an excellent shot; when he returns to the States, we plan to resume hunting mongooses together. Don't know if you would be interested, but you would be welcome to come!

There are lots of black people in Georgia. As you know, they were brought here in centuries past and offered opportunities in agriculture and the textile industry. I am sure you will fit in very well. I could introduce you to a successful realtor friend of mine.

Is it okay if she isn't black? She came here from Cambodia in the eighties. I can't understand a word she says, but she is clean and has wonderful manners.

The offer of the native costumes is very generous. I would be a big hit, wearing a getup like that down at the Water Buffalo Lodge! I would ask Betty her size, but she took off to go see the friend I was telling you about. God bless her; that woman is my world.

Barney Rubble
Stone Mountain, GA

"Opportunities in the agriculture and textile industries." That, my friends, is what I call "spin."

Having prepared Koffi for word from my friend Chiu, I wasted no time in having her contact him. Few experiences in this life are worse than being pestered by an excited realtor. I thought it was time for Koffi to find that out for himself.

Date: Wed, 12 Oct 2005 14:15:59 -0700 (PDT)
From: "Chiu Mai Dung"
Subject: Welcome Atlanta Area!
To: koffi_peabrain@hotmail.com

Dear Mr. Adams Sir!

Good day! Hope you not mind my contact you! My friend
Barney Rubbles give me your name. You look for house,
Atlanta/Stone Mountain area, he tell me.

Happy Dragon Realty Co. fifteen years Atlanta metroplex!
Residential, commercial, sale, rental . . . all same same. You
tell me what you want, I find. I serve you long time.

Please excuse English! American girl home with
mongonucreosis.

Chiu Mai Dung
Happy Dragon Realty Company
350 Spelman Lane SW
Atlanta, GA 30314-4399
404-794-xxxx

Mongonucreosis is a bitch.

I have no idea where I got the address and phone number
for Happy Dragon Realty Company. I think the phone
number came from an Atlanta strip club. Koffi clearly read
the e-mail, but he never replied to Chiu directly. A wise
choice. Acknowledging the existence of a realtor is like
making eye contact with a crackhead.

Koffi's emotions got the better of him.

From: "Adams Koffi" <koffi_peabrain@hotmail.com>
To: "Barney Rubble"

Subject: Re: GOODNEWS
Date: Thu, 13 Oct 2005 09:46:55 +0000

Barney-

You have written so well that I don't know where to start replying your mail but from the bottom of my heart I wish to thank you more especially for the love and trust you have shown me. Susan and myself has been married for 15yrs now although I'm much more older than she is but here age doesn't matter when it comes to choosing a life partner, is not like what we have in Europe and America where people get married in the night and get divorce in the morning but here, it is for life or no marriage at all.

I am getting ready to meet you face to face in your country as I will be going to your EMBASSY in our country to apply for VISA, I will keep you update as soon as I obtain the Visa and Please I will like to know if you do leave very close to any of the international air-port and if yes what is the name of the air port and the name of any nearby hotel in your neighbourhood.

Also do keep me posted as soon as the bank contacts you with more info and kindly furnish me with your mobile phone number for easy communication.

Best Regards

Koffi.

"Susan"? Didn't he say his wife's name was Barbara? I just caught that. He's a bigger liar than Barney, if that is possible.

Chiu Mai was still on the case. She smelled a commission,

and she was damn well going to get it. Unfortunately, she
had the wrong price range. And that limited her options.

Date: Thu, 13 Oct 2005 14:40:49 -0700 (PDT)
From: "Chiu Mai Dung"
Subject: Fine Atlanta Homes
To: koffi_peabrain@hotmail.com

Dear Mr. Adams Sir!

So sorry; American girl still sick. But I find several homes for
you.

Mr. Barney Rubbles tell me you have budget from 50,000-
80,000 dollar. Sadly must say, this somewhat low for Atlanta
area. Typical home price 200,000+ Lower cost homes always
have little problem I think. But I find some very acceptable
option. Paste link into browser to see.

http://tinyurl.com/d67kg [I wish this link still worked,
because this place was a true craphole]

House small, but roof fairly new. Price low due to presence of
pig farm across street. Wind usually from other direction.
Winter not so bad.

http://tinyurl.com/a4unr [This place was the kind of house
you would expect Ed Gein to use for storing bodies]

Attractive siding on this one. Several nice fruit tree. Property
discounted after cult murders; this many years ago and all but
three killers now in prison.

http://tinyurl.com/dy745 [A dump with a completely dead
lawn]

Excellent opportunity for homemaker with green thumb. House in fine shape, but lawn refuse to grow due to chemical spill. Topsoil replacement not expensive. Cheapest local landscape firm Lucky Family Tree & Sod, belong to my son Wei Kao Dung.

You feel comfortable with bigger budget, I have much more choices for you!

God bress.

Chiu Mai Dung
Happy Dragon Realty Company
350 Spelman Lane SW
Atlanta, GA 30314-4399
404-794-xxxx

His remarks to the contrary notwithstanding, Koffi did not seem very interested in snapping up any of these fine Atlanta-area homes.

From: "Adams Koffi" <koffi_peabrain@hotmail.com>
To: "Barney Rubble"
Subject: CONTACT THE BANK
Date: Fri, 14 Oct 2005 10:26:05 +0000

Dear Brother Barney,

I so much thank you for your effort in safe guarding a place for me to stay when i come in to US but the most important thing now is for us to make sure that this fund leaves africa to america unfarlingly before next week so you have try your possible best to contact the bank immediately so that this fund will leave immediately.

Brother Barney, Please this is very important at this juncture we need not to make any mistake now because earlier the better so you have to contact them and get back to me asap.

Koffi

Koffi was getting impatient, and Chiu wasn't getting any traction with him, so I had to think of a new tactic to delay him.

Date: Mon, 17 Oct 2005 13:10:31 -0700 (PDT)
From: "Barney Rubble"
Subject: Re: CONTACT THE BANK
To: "Adams Koffi" <koffi_peabrain@hotmail.com>

Dear Koffi:

I only have a minute to write. Something has come up and I will be away from my computer for a couple of days.

Don't ask me any questions. The less you know the better.

Chiu Mai wants to know if you would be interested in a duplex. I told her how the hell would I know, and to e-mail you herself. She is a nice lady but very persistent. She seems to have the wrong idea about your price range.

I will contact the damn bank again, although I must say they aren't making much effort to get our business. Here in America they give away toasters.

I am taking a short trip to Johannesburg. Please let me know if you have any idea how, while I am there, I can get my hands on an autoloading shotgun.

I decided that wasn't obvious enough, so I followed it immediately with this.

Date: Mon, 17 Oct 2005 13:13:29 -0700 (PDT)
From: "Barney Rubble"
Subject: Fwd: RUBBLE: MESSAGE FROM IBIZA
To: koffi_peabrain@hotmail.com

Dear Koffi:

To hell with it. I might as well show you why I am on my way to Africa.

Will check e-mail in a day or two.

I'll give that bitch "Buzz Lightyear." I am a peaceful man, but in Vietnam I had a big collection of pickled pinky toes.

Note: forwarded message attached.

Forwarded Message
Date: Mon, 17 Oct 2005 12:49:52 -0700 (PDT)
From: "ben joeff"
Subject: RUBBLE: MESSAGE FROM IBIZA
To: "Barney Rubble"

Plain Text Attachment

DEAR RUBBLES:

I PRESUME YOU HAVE RECOGNIZE THE ATTACHED PHOTO. IT IS THE TORSO OF YOUR LOVELY WIFE BETTY, WHO IS ENJOYING A HOLIDAY WITH ME ON SUNNY IBIZA. SHE

WIRED A SUBSTANTIAL SUM TO ME FROM YOUR INVESTMENT ACCOUNT, AND WE SPENT THE WEEKEND HERE AT THE EL DIVINO APARTMENTS [an actual resort in Ibiza], MAKING MIRTH AND FROLIC BY ALL POSSIBLE MODALITIES.

SHE WISHES ME TO INFORM YOU THAT SHE SHALL BE ACCOMPANYING ME TO JOHANNESBURG. SHE BELIEVES I INTEND TO MARRY HER, HOWEVER I SHALL RETURN HER TO YOU AS SOON AS I HAVE GOTTEN SUFFICIENT USE OF HER. SHE MIGHT BE WISE TO VISIT A PHYSICIAN, AS WE HAVE NOT BEEN USING CONNIES. [My little salute to Ali G.]

SHE MENTIONED YOUR NEED TO USE A MECHANICAL DEVICE HELD ON BY VELCRO AND INFORMED ME THAT SHE REFERS TO YOU AS "BUZZ LIGHTYEAR." YOU PROBABLY ARE NOT INTERESTED IN MY ADVICE BUT IF I WERE YOU I WOULD DROP THE BITCH AND FIND MYSELF SOME NEW CRUMPET.

YOUR WIFE'S TREACHERY MADE SUCH AN IMPRESSION ON MY THAT I HAD TO INCLUDE THIS SUGGESTION. ORDINARILY I WOULD SIGN OFF SIMPLY BY SAYING "BOLLOCKS".

BEN JOEFFUS, BARR.

Barney's troubles notwithstanding, Chiu Mai Dung was a closer, and she was determined to get some play.

Date: Tue, 18 Oct 2005 18:30:44 -0700 (PDT)
From: "Chiu Mai Dung"
Subject: Duprex
To: koffi_peabrain@hotmail.com

Dear Mr. Adams Sir!

Hope you are well. I try to speak to Mr. Barney Rubbles about you yesterday but he not in happy mood.

Was wondering if you might be interest in condo duplex instead of single-family home. Share home with nice neighbors, and cost less than real house. My family poor when come to US and find this excellent way to build equity while working way out of menial job.

I show you example. Please paste into browser window.

http://tinyurl.com/cvqk8 [A hole no self-respecting rat would inhabit]

This one much nicer inside than out. Please believe. Upstairs unit belong to nice man who work at home. He breed water moccasin for pet trade.

http://tinyurl.com/9kn85 [Paging Mr. Sanford . . .]

This one prettier and larger because area farther from town and cheaper. Close to outlet mall with many fast food restaurants where immigrant with no education can get foothold in US job market.

http://tinyurl.com/cfb3o [Satan is preparing a place just like this for Martha Stewart]

This one come on market last month after downstairs resident expire from Legionnaire Disease. Expect go-ahead from department of health any day now. Added bonus: furniture still in home, including almost-new mattress. Also clothing and water pik.

You send deposit and I nail one of these down for you! As fellow new American, I know you look forward to rescuing family from dirty backward country.

Chiu Mai Dung
Happy Dragon Realty Company
350 Spelman Lane SW
Atlanta, GA 30314-4399
404-794-xxxx

Koffi still didn't seem interested in Chiu's offerings, so I decided it was time for Ben to Kick things up a notch.

Date: Mon, 10 Oct 2005 11:21:00 -0700 (PDT)
From: "ben joeff"
Subject: Fwd: little tease for my sweet babboo
To:koffi_peabrain@hotmail.com

From Barrister Joeffus Ben Tel: +228-990-44-66

ADAMS YOU IGNORANT MAN I WANTED YOU TO SEE THAT YOUR EFFORTS HAVE COME TO NAUGHT. I ATTACH A PHOTO OF RUBBLE'S WIFE. I HAVE SEVERAL MORE LIKE IT. I HAVE RECEIVED FUNDS IN THE AMOUNT OF 3500 USD FROM HER SO FAR AND THE STUPID WOMAN WANTS TO MEET WITH ME IN A HOTEL IN IBIZA. SHE IS QUITE INFATUATED AND REFERS TO ME AS HER "NUBIAN LOVE GOD"

I ADVISE YOU TO CEASE ATTEMPTING TO CONTACT THESE PERSONS. YOU ARE ONLY MAKING A FOOL OF YOURSELF I SHALL SEND PHOTOS FROM IBIZA

Note: forwarded message attached.

Date: Mon, 10 Oct 2005 11:14:47 -0700 (PDT)
From: "betty rubble"
Subject: little tease for my sweet babboo
To: benjoeffuhoh@yahoo.com

Plain Text Attachment

hey sexy!!

it was fun IMin you last night!! barney had no clue he was
passed out on the sofa!!

i will try to get a webcam this week but i have to figure out
how to install it without barney knowing about it!! my cousin
Gertrude might help!! she drives a 4WD and changes her own
oil!!

i am attaching a little present for you!! do NOT open in front of
anyone there at your law office, K? it's very very special! i
hope you don't mind skinny girls!!

i have been lookin at vacation spots in your part of the world
and i think i could swing a weekend in ibiza!! my girlfriend
from college would cover for me and say i was visiting her.
she hates barney and says he is a "big fat bag of guts"!!

~~betty!!

Finally, Ben and Barney got a rise out of Koffi. He was so
upset he sat down to write an e-mail, in the middle of giving
his robe a fresh coat of Mop 'n' Glo.

From: "Adams Koffi" <koffi_peabrain@hotmail.com>
To: "Barney Rubble"
Subject: Re: CONTACT THE BANK
Date: Wed, 19 Oct 2005 12:31:10 +0000

Dear Brother Barney,

Please what have come over you that makes you to write to
me like that i have told you to do away with the mails of that
man but you and your wife continue to communicate with
him infact i don't understand what you meant by forwarding
that to me.

Moreover the way you are treating this offer now is not worth
expected from you have sent the application to the bank and
they have contacted you stating to you what is needed for the
fund to be transfered but up till now you have refuse to get
back to them, you are telling me that they are not making any
efforts while the ball is in your court.

Please Barney i want you to make it clear to me if you really
want to continue with this transaction or not since up till now
you have refuse to contact the bank then you are telling me
that you are going to Johannesburg that i should not ask you
question excuse me do you think we are playing or we are
into child's play don't you know that we are talking of million
of dollars (15 million US dollars).

Regarding to the house there is nothing i can do now untill
this fund is secured and tranfered to you ok.

Please for the last time you go ahead and contact the bank
immediately you recieve this email ok and get back to me asap
because this fund has to leave Africa to America this week
unfairlingly. Really i don't have idea of your travell to
johannesburg.

Koffi

Barney was a basket case. Koffi was no help at all! I guess
a little compassion was too much to expect!

Date: Thu, 20 Oct 2005 14:25:01 -0700 (PDT)
From: "Barney Rubble"
Subject: Re: CONTACT THE BANK
To: "Adams Koffi" <koffi_peabrain@hotmail.com>

Oh Jesus, Koffi. Oh Jesus. What have I done?

I am so sorry I brought you into this. I should never have told you. You were so kind to bring me in on this deal, and you say such thoughtful things in your e-mails, and look how I repay you. Flying off the handle in a jealous rage. God I am so sorry. Won't you forgive me? No, why should you, after what I've done? Why should anyone?

I was just so hurt. I thought Betty was the one, and then . . . that e-mail. I couldn't stop myself. I'm such a chump!!! I HATE MYSELF.

I found them in Sun City. You will probably read about it in the papers over there. No one saw me slip in and out. They were on the bed laughing and drinking champagne, and then there was blood everywhere, and I was running back to the car and then driving so fast I blistered my feet.

Oh, my sweet Betty. What I would give to have you back.

I am back in Georgia now. I contacted the bank. I don't know why the stupid bastards don't get back to me. I will re-send the e-mail. I don't give a rat's ass if I live or die. I just want you and your family to get that money. You can keep my share for all I care.

I need to get away. I'm going to spend the weekend in Frantic City with my friend Gazoo.

Keep this to yourself, my dear, dear friend. And give thanks to God for those faithful wives of yours.

It was sad, really. Barney had thought he had found his One True Love, and then he had learned different. But Koffi had apparently met his One True Love several dozen times. And each one had only cost him a few goats.

From: "Adams Koffi" <koffi_peabrain@hotmail.com>
To: "Barney Rubble"
Subject: Re: CONTACT THE BANK
Date: Fri, 21 Oct 2005 18:53:19 +0000

Dear Barney,

Have you really contact the bank for the shiftment of your fund?

Please get back to me ok.

Koffi

Barney had found solace in the company of his small green chum, the Great Gazoo. Perhaps you will remember Gazoo. I think he was from Mars. He was a little gay dude about two feet tall. He used to hover in the air and tell Fred and Barney how stupid they were. Anyway, it turns out he's a fool for casino gambling.

Date: Fri, 21 Oct 2005 13:59:16 -0700 (PDT)
From: "Barney Rubble"
Subject: Fwd: Perry Rubble
To: koffi_peabrain@hotmail.com

Dear friend Koffi:

I am e-mailing from the hotel in Frantic City. I feel somewhat better. Gazoo says hi. He won $35 playing pocket pool.

I am forwarding the e-mail I sent and re-sent to the bank. I
don't know what their danged problem is.

Am I supposed to use the regular mail? I have a phobia of
licking stamps.

Note: forwarded message attached. [SNIP—you've seen it.
Remember? The house on Charlatan Street?]

As I may have said before, these days, 419ers have gone
corporate. It used to be that when you heard from a Nigerian—I am using the term "Nigerian" generically here, even
though Koffi says he's from Togo—it was a lone boob on a
borrowed computer. These days, the successful Nigerians are
like pimps. They have stables of lesser Nigerians working for
them. That's actually true, even though you read it in this
ridiculous book. I assume the good Reverend is Koffi's pimp.
If the Reverend is Louis Farrakhan, Koffi is like the bow-
tied guys you see on Harlem street corners, selling newspa-
pers and bean pies.

From: "Adams Koffi" <koffi_peabrain@hotmail.com>
To: "Barney Rubble"
Subject: KEEP ME POSTED
Date: Mon, 24 Oct 2005 11:04:33 +0000

Dear Barney,

How are you today, hope all is well, Please have you been
able to hear from the bank once again please make sure you
get back to me and don't ever forget to forward to me
whatever message you recieved from them ok. Incase you
have not heared from them please try as much as possible to
call them on their phone +228-927 3188.

Make sure in your phone call you ask of the Bank Director Rev.Edmond Jean-Claude then ask him what is delaying the transfer of your fund ok, you know i could have done that by myself but due to the nature of the inheritance i don't want them to know my involvement as i told you earlier on this is between me and you ok. So you do that and get back to me because time is no longer our friend and we have to make sure that this fund lives Africa to America this week unfairlingly, or you go ahead and call me on my private line +228-9222238.

Looking forward to hearing from you.

Koffi

Koffi believed I had blown Betty in half with an autoloading shotgun. He believed I had a friend named Gazoo who made money playing pocket pool. I was at wit's end. What could I tell him now to top all that? The stress of the challenge drove Barney to seek relief in religion. And he called in some help from Gazoo and another member of the Hanna-Barbera team.

Date: Sun, 30 Oct 2005 14:40:56 -0800 (PST)
From: "Barney Rubble"
Subject: Re: KEEP ME POSTED
To: "Adams Koffi" <koffi_peabrain@hotmail.com>

Dear Koffi:

Honestly, sometimes I think this whole enterprise is cursed. Many times I have wondered if God is getting even with me for that time when I was thirteen and confused by unfamiliar urges and I did that thing to the neighbor's cat. I have sent my information to the bank twice, and I have not heard one danged word.

I will send the information a third time. I have to send it anyway, because . . . I am so scared to tell you this. You have been so kind to involve me in this, and you have been willing to do business with my good friend Chiu Mai, and now I am afraid that you will make fun of me or think that I have done gone crazy. I hope you will not break faith with me, because even though my life is basically crap in a handbasket I want more than anything to see you and your family make it to Georgia and move into that duplex Chiu keeps yammering about.

I have to send the information again because it has changed. For you see, this week I was with my friend Gazoo Sathyavagiswaran at his place of worship, the Stone Mountain Temple of Karmic Fatuity. He took me there hoping to share the peace he had found by adhering to the Hare Krishna philosophy. Perhaps you have heard of these people. They achieve inner peace and enlightenment by shaving their heads and selling people books at airports.

I was quite taken by their teachings, and I have decided to give it a shot. I have taken a yogi, or holy man, as a mentor. His name is Max Baer, Jr., and he used to have an appliance repair shop until he drank up all the profits and ended up in the gutter, where the Krishnas found him while they were chanting in front of a T.G.I. Friday's.

Anyway, Yogi Baer says I need a complete transformation, so on his recommendation I have taken the Hindi name Dabbadoo Roganjosh. I filled out the name change papers this week. From now on, I will only be corresponding from the address dabbadooxxx@yahoo.com.

The change of name serves two purposes. It signifies that I am serious about putting my old life behind me and giving this new religion a shot. It will hopefully also make it harder for me to be tracked down by the authorities in South Africa.

Yogi Baer said I should show my commitment to Krishna by donating five thousand dollars to the temple, so I raided my retirement account.

I will let you know if those idiots at the bank ever get back to me. Until then, may the truths of Bhagavata be revealed unto you, my friend.

D. Roganjosh
Stone Mountain, GA

I don't have the slightest clue what the truths of Bhagavata are. I found that on the Internet. I have a feeling they have something to do with giving all your money to the Hare Krishnas. I figured even a doofus from B.F. Togo would have some idea who Yogi Bear was. But I was mistaken. The Reverend had no idea. In fairness, he is a reverend and not a fakir or a swami or a poobah or whatever sort of person it is who runs a Hare Krishna temple. And I doubt he had watched the O.J. trial.

I really did make them send mail to that new Yahoo! address.

Date: Mon, 31 Oct 2005 20:01:35 +0100
Subject: +228-9273188
From: "btcil" <BTCI1@pepelepew.net>
To: "mr_bernard_rubble"
Attn: Mr Barney Rubble,

Dear Sir,

We acknowledge the receipt of your email but meanwhile your former name has been used already for your documents as the bonafide next of kin to your cousine Perry Rubble. Notwithstanding your new name shall be used for further documentation when the transfer shall be made, meanwhile you go ahead and contact us via telephone for more clarification and information our number is +228-927-3188 immediately.

Rev. Edmond Jean-Claude

As for Koffi, he was not a judgmental guy, and he had little to say about my sudden conversion.

From: "Adams Koffi" <koffi_peabrain@hotmail.com>
To: "Barney Rubble"
Subject: CALL THE BANK
Date: Tue, 01 Nov 2005 08:27:28 +0000

Dear Barney,

I really understand your mail but the most important thing now is how this money will be transfered? I believe the bank shall get back to you this week unfairlingly and you must endeavour to call the director of the bank as I earlier on told you on my last mail ok. Here is their number +228-927-3188

Koffi

Here is where I'll get in trouble for being a bigot. If I'm not in trouble already for the Tarzan references. I am sure that in Asia, Eastern religions are totally above board and serious about helping people attain Nirvana or Total Consciousness or the Perfect 30-Minute Tantric Orgasm or whatever. But here in the United States, they are rackets even worse than the 700 Club.

Let me tell you about my experience with Buddhism. I dated a lunatic for a while, and she was an atheist, and one day she decided she wanted to be a Buddhist. She got some pamphlets from the gay couple who owned the house in which she rented a room. They were Buddhists. As I understand it, Buddhism is big with gays, probably because Buddha never said anything about roasting them with fire and brimstone.

Anyway, before she looked at the literature, she asked me to check it out, knowing full well that I was a Christian and that I regarded American Buddhists with the highest degree of cynicism and amusement. I mean, come on. Steven Seagal is a Buddhist.

So anyway, I grab a pamphlet, and as God (the real One, not Buddha) is my witness, it was all about a bitter lawsuit between the gay couple's sect and some other sect that had clearly fallen short of enlightenment. I don't recall the basis of the suit. Maybe they wanted to enjoin the other cult from using Buddha's likeness on the packaging for a line of biodegradable love oils and organic condoms. But the gist of the literature was that the other outfit was full of unspiritual clods who were not At One With The Universe. And they were going to get theirs. Not by being reincarnated as dung beetles or pubic lice or telemarketers, but by being gutted by the first cult's lawyers, who were the farthest thing from enlightened.

I thought she had already read this stuff, and that she had given it to me for a laugh, but I was wrong. And I learned that I was wrong. As soon as I started laughing. You men know how that works.

Anyway, the Hare Krishnas are about the same as Buddhists, and their church is a racket, and I don't care who knows I feel that way. I'm not afraid of a bunch of scrawny vegetarians in orange bedsheets. I eat meat and carry a knife.

The Hare Krishnas saw themselves, correctly, as direct competitors to Koffi and the dear Reverend. Even though they were fictional.

I created a Yogi Baer Yahoo address. Please note the signature he placed at the end of his message. I decided to mention sweat lodges and spirit guides again.

Date: Fri, 4 Nov 2005 11:06:24 -0800 (PST)
From: "Max Baer" <yogi_baerxxx@yahoo.com>
Subject: Re: Fwd: +2289273188
To: BTCl1@pepelepew.net

Blessings of the Llama be upon you.

Dabbadoo Roganjosh, whom you useded to know as Barny Rubble give me this emails address. As you by now know, Mr. Roganjosh has now becomed a follower of His Divine Grace A. C. Bhaktivedanta Swami Prabhupada. Perhaps you have seened the Divine One's photo on the cover of books what are made available at your local airport.

Like all new Vedic disciples, Dabbadoo has agreeded to renounst lowly stuff such as the pursuits of wealth and trolling for skank. Because now advancing the goals of Hare Krishna is the importantest thing in Dabbadoo's life, he has agreed to submit all his financial decisions to approval by me, his mentor and what you might call a sort of "personal Jesus."

Being as that is the case, you will now have to send all communications through me here at my appliance shop. I will bring your messages before the weekly Council of Yogis and after the usual dancing we will vote on whether to go on with your scheme or merely empty Disciple Dabbadoo's accounts into our treasury.

In all seriousness and candor, the latter is by far more likelier.

I will relay whatever you has to say to Disciple Dabbadoo, although right now he is spending a couple days in our Sweat Lodge where it is hoped that he will have visions and encounter his Spirit Guide or Garam Masala, a being which takes the form of an animal and helps true seekers find their way to Nirvana. I personally installed the space heaters in that lodge, because I was able to get them wholesale. If those silicone-filled baseboard jobs hardwired to 220 won't give you a vision, you just ain't trying.

Dabbadoo was hoping for a really cool guide like a tiger, but I told him to be grateful and respectful even if it were something less impressive such as a goose or even a wiener dog.

Yours in all serenity and chastity,

Yogi Baer

Barney Rubble wrote:

[SNIP-forwarded message from bank]

Baer Small Appliance: servicing all Maytag and Magic Chef models since 1991. Call 404-892-xxxx.

Smarter than your average repairman!

Hare Krishna, Hare Krishna, Krishna Krishna, Hare Hare, Hare Booboo, Hare Booboo, Booboo Booboo, Hare Hare.

After that, I got a long rest. But a couple of months later, I could not resist checking to see if Koffi remembered me. Surely he wouldn't answer a new e-mail.

Date: Tue, 10 Jan 2006 09:06:36 -0800 (PST)
From: "Barney Rubble"
Subject: Re: CALL THE BANK
To: "Adams Koffi" <koffi_peabrain@hotmail.com>

Dear Koffi:

I just escaped from the Temple. When I told them I wanted to leave and take my funds with me, they locked me in a broom closet. I managed to choke Yogi Baer with my manacle chain during a potty break, and I lit out through a bathroom window. I hope they reincarnate him as some sort of parasite that lives in a pig's behind.

I have had it with rice and chanting. Let me know if you still want to do business.

B. Rubble
Parts Unknown

No WAY would he answer that. No WAY. Impossible. After "Hare Booboo Hare Booboo"? Come on.

From: "Adams Koffi" <koffi_peabrain@hotmail.com>
To: "Barney Rubble"
Subject: CALL THE BANK
Date: Wed, 11 Jan 2006 09:20:53 +0000

Dear Barney,

Thanks for your mail and the contents duly noted. You better go ahead and contact the bank's director Rev. Edmond Jean-

Claude asking them the position of your deceased cousine fund ok. Their email address still remain BTCI1@pepelepew.net while their new phone number +2289491807 you can still contact them via telephone for more information.

Koffi

Can you believe me when I say that sometimes these e-mails make me cry? I laugh so hard I have to get up from the computer and go lie on the living room floor.

It was too much. I had to set it aside for a while, because I couldn't stand it.

But then I started in again.

Date: Mon, 30 Jan 2006 06:49:23 -0800 (PST)
From: "Barney Rubble"
Subject: I Have Returned
To: BTCI1@pepelepew.net

Dear Rev. Whatever:

This is me, Barney Rubble. You will recall that I was efforting to help your pal Koffi Adams to extract funds from your country, prior to my ill-advised decision to become a Hare Krishna. As Koffi has probably told you, I had a change of heart, choked out my Hare Krishna mentor, Mr. Yogi Baer, and escaped from the temple via a bathroom window.

I am done with heathen religions and am now ready to talk turkey. In fact, after months of an insipid vegetarian diet, I get pretty excited just typing the word "turkey."

Please do not e-mail me under my previous name, Mr. Dabbadoo Roganjosh. Due to the violent nature of my escape, I am concerned that the authorities will be checking to see if I log in using that identity. Alas, poor Yogi. I knew him well.

Let's get the ball rolling. I will stay in touch as best I can,
given as I am currently on the run from the law. It is my
understanding that Ranger Smith has been assigned to my
case.

Would you happen to know if your country has an extradition
treaty with the US?

Barney Rubble
Parts Unknown

I also rekindled my warm relationship with my great
friend Koffi.

Date: Mon, 30 Jan 2006 06:58:59 -0800 (PST)
From: "Barney Rubble"
Subject: Re: CALL THE BANK
To: "Adams Koffi" <koffi_peabrain@hotmail.com>

Dear, dear Koffi:

Thank you so much for getting back to me, after the way I
abandoned you for a screwy cult run by a fat greasy foreigner
in an orange nightgown. Your patience and kindness
overwhelm me.

I apologize for using the term "foreigner" in a derogatory
fashion, knowing that it applies to you and your lovely family,
but my nerves are somewhat frazzled, as I have spent the last
two weeks sleeping in a Goodwill collection bin, while I wait to
see if the authorities connect me with the apparent demise of
Yogi Baer.

I am waiting around for your friend the reverend to respond to
my e-mail. I thought I should ask if you are still interested in
buying property in Georgia. I called my friend Chiu Mai the

other day, and she says that with the bird flu scare and all, beautiful homes near poultry farms are selling very cheap. At least I think that's what she said. She has trouble with verb tenses and certain consonants and cannot pronounce the letter "R." It is completely possible she said they were selling sheep.

Although that would not make sense.

B. Rubble
No Address

Koffi had forgiven me, and the bank was anxious to follow suit. For a nominal fee.

Date: Wed, 1 Feb 2006 11:18:46 +0100
Subject: REACTIVATION FEE
From: "btci1" <BTCI1@pepelepew.net>
To: "mr_bernard_rubble"

Attn Mr Barney Rubble,

Dear Sir,

Following the board of directors meeting hold on your behalf and also your application being submitted since last year you are advise to send amount of $500 to our office for the reactivation of your cousin's account Mr Perry Rubble.

The account has been dominant since several years and you being the bonafide next of kin to the decease you are directed to send the money within 72hours as to enable us expediate actions on your behalf.

The money are to send through any western union or money gram available to you and with the name of our casheir

NAME:MR IKECHUKWU ADIGHIOGU

ADDRESS: 12 RUE DU BAGUIDA
LOME-TOGO.

We anticipate for your understanding and co-operation
towards this regard.

Please do contact the undersigned for further
enquiries/proceedures.

Rev. Edmond Jean Claude
Director of Foreign Remmitance
Diamond Deposit and Financier bank plc
Lome-Togo

Again, these idiots were pushing me to come to issue.
About half the work of dealing with 419ers is stalling. I
thought of an idea that would buy me time. I created my
own Koffi Adams address and sent Barney the following
message.

Date: Wed, 1 Feb 2006 16:30:02 +0000 (GMT)
From: "Koffi Adams" <koffiadamsxxxx8@yahoo.co.uk>
Subject: from koffi: Fox in the Henhouse
To: "Barney Rubble"

Brother Barney:

I am hoping this email will not cause you disturbment. I must
ask that you cease contacting me at my hotmail address. My
associate, Rev.Edmond Jean-Claude, has been intercepting
my communications and attempting to deal directly with my
business contacts, so I have created this new address to
confound him.

Brother Barney I am going to handle our business personally, so please disregard all communications from the Rev. especially if he requests funds. I am sorry to say that Rev. Jean-Claude has become severely addicted to hashish and has been cheating kindhearted Americans in order to buy his filthy drugs.

Kindly send a message to my old address saying all is well and whatnot and then I will need to you to wire me 750 USD in order to reactivate Cousin Perry's account. I shall provide the information in a seperate email.

This is highly embarrassing. Please do not break faith with me over this scoundrel's tomfoolery.

Also, I was wondering if you would like a beautiful togolese hat.

With Love

Koffi

You're with me, right? You understand that I wrote that. And I "accidentally" forwarded it to the bank, hoping the Reverend would kick Koffi in the ass so hard he ended up in Georgia without benefit of an airline ticket. Koffi was still in the dark. His characteristic state.

From: "Adams Koffi" <koffi_peabrain@hotmail.com>
To: "Barney Rubble"
Subject: HAVE YOU HEARED FROM THE BANK
Date: Wed, 01 Feb 2006 22:23:50 +0000

Dear Barney,

Have you heared from the bank please incase you have heared from them do not hesistate to forward their message to me ok.

Koffi

Barney wasn't fooled! He had been told exactly what to do.

Date: Wed, 1 Feb 2006 08:47:19 -0800 (PST)
From: "Barney Rubble"
Subject: Re: CALL THE BANK
To: "Adams Koffi" <koffi_peabrain@hotmail.com>

Dear Koffi:

All is well and whatnot. The situation is under control, and your emails are well understood.

Barney

Evidently, the bank and the good Reverend contacted Koffi about the impostor's e-mail.

From: "Adams Koffi" <koffi_peabrain@hotmail.com>
To: "Barney Rubble"
Subject: CONFIRM URGENTLY
Date: Thu, 02 Feb 2006 15:48:18 +0000

Dearest Barney,

How are you today hope your fine? Please my dear good friend i want to bring to your notice that something fishy have been going on in our back regarding some people who have been working tirelessly to have your cousin fund diverted for thier own deadly interest and benefits. Could you believe that I was invited by the bank authority for a meeting of their board of directors and trustees, in this meeting i got to understand that there has been the existence of ghost staffs that have been working against the bank interest and mode of operations.

I happens to find out that two bank workers that i earlier approached to assist me with directives and guidelines on how we will secure this fund under bank custody was among the sacked ghost workers of the bank, ever did I know that they pretended to assist me without knowing that they were interest in getting some information about the fund so that they will have it diverted. I thank God that your mail to the bank have aroused the awareness to them which made them to carry out urgent investigations even though your mail rendered insults to their director image but it made to noticed that it was this sacked ghost workers that are behind what is going on and as was agreed upon, they will soon be apprehended. Please my dear good friend, it is said that united we stand and divided we fall, right now we have to be strongly united and trusted to each other for us to succeed.

Imagine that this idots went to the extent to tamper my phone line thereby tapping my calls and diverting it as well. Is now that i also realised the complain of most the clients that usually come to my chambers complaining that each time they call me, that i will pass new instruction outside what we originally discussed and agreed. Please my friend, to curtail this ugly thing that is going underground behind our back, i have just secured a new phone number (+2289462004) for security of this transaction, i advised you to call me immediately you receive this mail so that you will confirm this number to me. Again, the amount the bank demanded to reactivate the account is $500 and not $750 as those idiots are requesting from you. Please you mustn't do anything without my order so that an unwarranted idiots wouldn't take your money without been the appropriate authority authorised to such money. I really hoped that this mail finds you well satisfactory and duly understood. Lastly, i have pleaded to the bank authority on your behalf but they insisted that you must apologies to them, so i therefore plead to you to do that immediately without any delay for our own betterment. I really glad that the bank itself are ready to take adequate measures against these sacked ghost workers and have also maintain proper security measures.

Thanks and God bless. I look forward for your quick confirmation.

Best regards,
Koffi Adams.

Good God, man, does your pimp pay you by the keystroke? Is there any way you could manage to write me a LONGER e-mail next time?

I should also mention Yogi Baer's effort to enlist Koffi's help. He sent Koffi this message:

Date: Wed, 1 Feb 2006 08:41:08 -0800 (PST)
From: "Max Baer" <yogi_baerxxxxx@yahoo.com>
Subject: B. Rubble
To: koffi_peabrain@hotmail.com
Dear Adams:

I am writing to find out if you can assist me in locating the whereabouts of Y. Roganjosh, formerly known as Bernard Rubble. The ungrateful basterd choked me unconcious on the floor of the mens can here at the temple, and I have sent the fuzz after him. The temple is offering a reward of $75 cash money or a free copy of Swami Pruphapahdamanapad's four-

volume work "Principles of Enlightenment and Offshore
Banking for Dummies."

Y. Baer

**Baer Small Appliance: servicing all Maytag and Magic Chef
models since 1991. Call 404-892-xxxx.**

Smarter than your average repairman!

**Hare Krishna, Hare Krishna, Krishna Krishna, Hare Hare,
Hare Booboo, Hare Booboo, Booboo Booboo, Hare Hare.**

That one didn't get me a response. The folks at the bank
soon got in touch, with an explanation for the bogus e-mail.

Date: Thu, 2 Feb 2006 16:00:35 +0100
Subject: WARNING/ADVICE
From: "btci1" <BTCI1@pepelepew.net>
To: "mr_bernard_rubble"
Attn: Barney Rubble,

Following your embarrasing mail received here in our bank,
series of varifications and investigations were conducted and
we were able to fished out the culprits engaged in this acts in
order to tarnish the image of this bank and generally the
reputation of our dearly respected, highly esteem and straight
forward director in the person of Rev. Edmond Jean Claude,
who has been in charge of this bank for many years now
without any bad record.

What prompted this impersonifications is that, at the end of
last year, our bank conducted some investigations regarding
ghost staffs who consituted hooligans to our bank image by
diverting and embezzeling customers fund herein our bank
custody and falsification of documents with our bank name

without the awareness of the authority, after they were duly fished out, the director then gave order to get them flushed out and sacked. Since this action was taken, they have been a torn to us, this prompted the bank authority to pass a new law, rules and regulations that now guides this bank, that on no account or any reason should our bank website /information be given out except authorized by the authority.

We also wished to inform you that a board of directors/trustees meeting were held today here in our bank with the invitation of Barrister Koffi Adams as he was present during this meeting. On this note, we are warning you for your own goodness and interest to be careful and make sure you rely and hold your trust to this bank if you want your cousin fund released and transferred directly to your account without any embargo. We hereby request you to tender an apology letter to this bank for the impersonification on our bank image else we shall hencefort terminate further proceedings and have your consin fund transferred into the account of our high government authority for probing on the origin of this fund.

Conclusively, our able director, Rev. Edmond Jean Claude is not a drug addit and doesn't even take alcohol to be precise. We the retained staffs of this bank adviced you to tender your sincere apology directly to Rev. Edmond Jean Claude by calling him on phone (00228-9491807). Once he accepts your apology will further proceedings commence following his order. We wish you the best of luck and understanding towards this regard.

Yours Faithfully,
Mrs. Jarvita Daniel
Secretary.

Barney was still on the spot. They wanted that money. I thought it might be time for him to get involved with another cult. Naturally, I thought of Tinseltown's favorite sawed-off mental case, Tom Cruise.

Date: Fri, 17 Feb 2006 11:24:08 -0800 (PST)
From: "Barney Rubble"
Subject: Re: WARNING / ADVICE
To: "btci1" <BTCI1@pepelepew.net>

Dear Juanita:

I would like to apologize for being taken in by that bum. I am sorry for not getting back to you sooner. I was hiding out down by the stockyards when I saw some Hare Krishna goons nosing around, and I knew vegetarians had no business being there, so I hopped a freight and wound up in Juarez, Mexico.

I had to hitchhike home. It appears that the law is not after me and the cult nutties have given up searching for me, so you and Mr. Adams may reach me at this e-mail address from now on. Although for the next couple of days I will be at a retreat offered by the Scientology people. They say Tom Cruise will be there.

Barney Rubble
Stone Mountain, GA

I also kept Koffi in the loop.

Date: Fri, 17 Feb 2006 11:32:43 -0800 (PST)
From: "Barney Rubble"
Subject: Re: YOUR RESPONSE
To: "Adams Koffi" <koffi_peabrain@hotmail.com>

Dear Brother Koffi:

I am so sorry I let that dirtball convince me he was you. He said the bank was trying to screw you, and well, I guess you get the idea.

As I explained to Mrs. Jarvis from the bank, I am now back at my normal residence, after an unintended junket out of the country. I assume the bank shall get back to me shortly, and we can proceed, as soon as I get myself E-metered and lose a few of these body thetans. My new friends advise me that I should be able to unload twenty or thousand this weekend. More, if I am willing to submit to a colonic.

God forgive me, I did enjoy administering frontier justice to Yogi Baer.

B. Rubble
Stone Mountain, GA

God bless those wonderful people at the bank. They accepted my apology for being duped by their former employees, and they were willing to take my money.

Date: Sat, 18 Feb 2006 15:30:18 +0100
Subject: FROM:BTCI
From: "btci1" <BTCI1@pepelepew.net>
To: "mr_bernard_rubble"
Date: 18th Febuary, 2006.

OUR REF;BTCI/TG0 4120
P;&nbs

Attn: Barney Rubble,

We are here in acknowledgement to the receipt of your apology mail dated 17th Febuary, 2006, we are hereby notifying you that your apology have been accepted by our able director general of this bank in the person of Rev.Edmond Jean Claude and the entire staffs.

We also guarantee you that your interest is protected as you transact with us and we promise you successful transfer of your fund directly to your domain destination account as soon our banking proceedures and requirement are completed by you without any hold

For further proceed, you are adviced to send to our bank immediately the sum amount of $500 for effective activation of your dormant account here in our bank as to enable us transfer your fund. The amount is payable through western union money transfer/moneygram money transfer using our bank cashier name below as the receipient.

NAME: MR.IKECHUKWU ADIGHOGU

ADDRESS: LOME-TOGO.

Please do not hesitate to contact the undersigned for further proceed/enquiries/assistance.

Yours Faithfully,
Mr.Edwin.Bonga.Paul.
Director Foreign Remittance Operation.

Koffi was beginning to sound incoherent. Perhaps Barney had driven him to try hashish, himself.

From: "Adams Koffi" <koffi_peabrain@hotmail.com>
To: "Barney Rubble"
Subject: Expecting to hear from you as quickly as possible
Date: Sat, 18 Feb 2006 16:47:52 +0000

Dearest Barney,

Thanks for your mail well received and i really thank for your understanding. Right now, i believe you will proceed further with the bank so that the money can get transferred to your account for our own splitting and not to evil doers that wanted to get you convinced so that they will use that opportunity to divert the fund to an unknown destination and have it shared. Am very much happy that the bank have sacked all those bandits and the bank i already to deal with them for try to tarnish their bank image and that of their director.

Please you to proceed ahead with the bank and make sure that proceedures are expediated for the successful transfer of the fund into your account. I also request that you give me a call as soon as you get this mail. Again, do not hesitate to do whatever the bank ask you to do because the power to have the money transferred is in their hand and as such, you must be co-operative with them. I really wished to thank you again for your understanding and co-operation with me as your partner. Have a nice weekend and God bless.

Sincerely Yours,
Koffi Adams.

Barney was cool with that. He understood the problems employers face these days.

Date: Mon, 20 Feb 2006 08:39:05 -0800 (PST)
From: "Barney Rubble"
Subject: Re: Expecting to hear from you as quickly as possible
To: "Adams Koffi" <koffi_peabrain@hotmail.com>

Dear Koffi:

I sympathize with your bank's personnel problems. It is impossible to get good help these days because prospective hires are all sullen tattooed slackjaws who watch MTV and think the world owes them a living.

Mrs. Jarvis said the bank's problem was caused by "ghost staffs." That went right over my head, but whoever it was who said Reverend Claude was a dope fiend, he ought to be tied to a stake and flogged, and they ought to make the other raggedy-ass slackjaws line up and watch. We can't do that in America anymore, which is a pity. But maybe you can get away with it over in Togo.

The Scientology retreat was very restful and informative. I got a free massage and some counseling and while I was at a picnic, they pointed out a guy who they claimed was Tom Cruise. I think they were pulling my leg, however, because he was kind of a runt and appeared to be light in the loafers.

I am communicating with the bank. I mentioned the deal to the Scientology folks, and they suggested I hang on for a week or so before sending money, because they might have investment suggestions of their own. I plan to comply, if you don't mind, because I think I can get a couple more free massages out of them, and they have offered to rid me of a few thousand more thetans on a complimentary basis. It is my understanding that this treatment is ordinarily quite expensive.

Anyway, I will take that up with the bank right now.

B.R.

I didn't know if Tom Cruise and his imaginary aliens were enough to put off the bank, so I decided to ask for more information regarding the wire transfer.

Date: Mon, 20 Feb 2006 08:55:02 -0800 (PST)
From: "Barney Rubble"
Subject: Re: FROM:BTCI
To: "btci1" <BTCI1@pepelepew.net>

Dear Paul:

It was very gracious of the bank to accept my apology, although I believe their former employees caused the problem. I have read that African law is somewhat less restrictive than American law; if that is truly the case I would suggest you give these ne'er-do-wells a painful beating. That will discourage them from interfering with your business in the future, in addition to affording you a good deal of satisfaction.

Regarding your Western Union instructions, is it really that simple? Do you only need a name and a city? No street address? I have sent money to folks here in the U.S., and they made me provide no end of useless information about the receiving parties. I am concerned that another Ed Paul could show up and nab the money. Perhaps one of the miscreants who pretended to be Koffi Adams. Then I would be out $500, you would not receive the money, and your former employees would no doubt be out drunk in a ditch somewhere.

It will be a few days before I can comply, anyway. I have recently become acquainted with persons involved in the Church of Scientology, and they have offered to provide me with free services if I hold off on investing money elsewhere for a week or so. I can't pass up a deal like that. After that, however, we should be good to go.

B. Rubble
Stone Mountain, GA

And that, best beloved, is where I left them. Their latest e-mails are waiting on Yahoo's servers. I'll come up with something new to tell them, Buddha and Tom Cruise willing.